Disabling the School-to-Prison Pipeline

Critical Issues in Disabilities and Education

Series Editor: Eric Shyman, St. Joseph's College

The social, legal, and political history of persons with disabilities in the United States as well as internationally has been significant, especially in the areas of social justice, civil rights, and cultural inclusion. This series will focus on various critical perspectives on issues involving the social, political, and cultural experiences of people with disabilities. Manuscripts in this series will address topics such as: (1) legal developments (such as issues with the Americans with Disabilities Act, Individuals with Disabilities Education Act, Education for All, and others) at both the national and international level; (2) social and cultural models of disability and its outcome on the inclusion and/or exclusion of individuals with disabilities; (3) the benefits and challenges of the current educational system for children and adolescents with disabilities, including specific methodologies and categories of students (e.g., educational approaches for students with Autism Spectrum Disorder, inclusive education for students with disabilities, etc.); (4) philosophical perspectives of special education/education for students with disabilities; (5) issues regarding transitional support services and approaches to community support for adults with disabilities. This series would be open to scholars representing education, psychology, sociology, philosophy, human relations, business and management, cultural anthropology, speech and language pathology, and medical sciences (among others). Manuscripts published in this series would be appropriate for use in scholarship and coursework at colleges and universities, as well as be written in a way to be accessible and appealing to a general intellectual audience.

Titles in the Series:

Disabling the School-to-Prison Pipeline: The Relationship Between Special Education and Arrest, by Laura Vernikoff

Contemplating Dis/Ability in Schools and Society: A Life in Education, by David J. Connor

Reconceptualizing Disability in Education, by Luigi Iannacci

Disabling the School-to-Prison Pipeline

The Relationship between Special Education and Arrest

Laura Vernikoff

LEXINGTON BOOKS
Lanham • Boulder • New York • London

Published by Lexington Books
An imprint of The Rowman & Littlefield Publishing Group, Inc.
4501 Forbes Boulevard, Suite 200, Lanham, Maryland 20706
www.rowman.com

6 Tinworth Street, London SE11 5AL, United Kingdom

British Library Cataloguing in Publication Information Available

Library of Congress Cataloging-in-Publication Data

Library of Congress Control Number: 2021933346

ISBN: 978-1-7936-2417-8 (cloth)
ISBN: 978-1-7936-2419-2 (pbk)
ISBN: 978-1-7936-2418-5 (electronic)

Contents

A Note from the Series Editor

The purpose of the *Critical Issues in Disabilities and Education* series published by Lexington Books is to provide a venue within which topics that fall outside of the mainstream research focus can be given voice to greater readership. While special education, the most common moniker for teaching students with various exceptionalities or dis/abilities, receives much attention in the popular empirical literature, there is considerably less attention paid to counter-narratives involving the social constructions of and social responses to the actually lived lives of individuals with disabilities. It is the goal of this series to provide the field with increased access to a collection of legitimate scholarly works exploring these issues from a depth and breadth not available elsewhere.

In *Disabling the School-to-Prison Pipeline: The Relationship Between Special Education and Arrest* Laura Vernikoff takes a deep dive into one of the most pernicious but under-regarded scourges of the Disability Rights Movement: the deep-seated racism and ethnocentrism that allows the perpetuation of a two-tiered segregated system, which excludes first by race, and then by disability. Her exploration, though accessible, is not simplistic. Instead of relying solely on truthful but easily dismissed tropes based out of identity politics or compelling, if not theatrical, anecdotal evidence, Vernikoff triangulates her investigation through an in-depth analysis of extant research, interpretation of data from her own well-designed mixed methods study and relating these findings to deepen her understanding of her own experiences in the classroom.

Using both a hyperopic approach in examining the School-to-Prison-Pipeline (STPP) at a national level as well as a myopic investigation focusing on the specific system in New York City, Vernikoff allows the reader a deep and honest look at how these consequential issues of race, ethnicity, and disability are perpetuated by a deeply flawed system, and how we, as individual teachers contribute to it on a daily basis with our own well-intentioned though biased and misguided culturally dominant practices.

If there is one true gift provided by this work, however, it is the place of deep care, compassion, and desire for genuine change from which it comes. This perspective is made clear through the attention paid to the most important players in the story: the students themselves. By giving a real voice to these students in a safe environment free from social and political consequences, Laura Vernikoff allows an uncensored and unmitigated view into their perceptions and perspectives, thus providing them a true means of liberation: the right to tell their own story.

This book would be important to include in any education course, undergraduate or graduate, or for any form of professional development regardless of whether the particular school or school system serves students of color or not. This is a book that is steeped in one of the harsher realities of American school culture, but one that must not go disregarded any longer. Laura Vernikoff's work is an excellent place to start.

Eric Shyman, Ed.D.
Editor, Critical Issues in Disabilities and Education

List of Tables

Acknowledgments

This book would not be possible without the help and support of many more amazing people than I have space to name here. I am grateful to my amazing dissertation committee, who helped make this a much more rigorous and ethical study than it would have been otherwise: Michael G. Wilson, Michelle Knight-Manuel, David J. Connor, and Elizabeth Tipton. Many thanks also to Lin Goodwin for your continued mentorship, and to Carolyn Riehl for expanding my researcher horizons. Thank you to Nancy Lesko and Srikala Naraian for all of your guidance and help over the years, too. I am also extremely lucky to have worked with many amazing scholars on research teams over the years to improve my research and academic writing skills.

Many thanks to Eric Shyman and the anonymous reviewer who read drafts and made helpful suggestions. This book is much improved from your input. Thank you to Acquisitions Editor Holly Buchanan for helping me throughout this process.

This book would, of course, not be possible without the contributions of the young participants who generously gave their time to speak with me during particularly challenging times in their lives. Many thanks, also, to the adults who helped me recruit participants despite the pressures of their demanding jobs. Thank you to the New York City Department of Education, New York State Education Department, and New York University Research Alliance for making data available for this and other research projects.

I am fortunate to come from a large extended family of educators and people who work toward equity and justice for people with disabilities. Special thanks to my favorite father, Steven Vernikoff, for typing up my very first stories for me when I was a little girl, and also for all of the conversations about disability rights and disability advocacy over the years. Thanks to my aunt Sharon O'Connor for sending me her first-day-of-school resources for my first-ever day of teaching, and to my aunt Maureen O'Connor for being my first-ever interview participant. Many thanks also to Fredda Rosen for the conversations and connections. Thanks to the rest of my extended family for all of the love and support!

Finally, I owe a huge debt to several people who passed away while I was working on this study. I am grateful to my mother, Barbara O'Connor for "deprogramming" me when I was a little girl and we watched TV together so that I didn't believe everything I heard and so, so much more. My grandfather, Abe Vernikoff, always wanted to know if I had enough money during graduate school, then asked me to send him some if I said that I did. My aunt Judy Vernikoff kept me updated on what everyone in the family was doing and never, ever forgot a birthday, anniversary, or other important event. My former student Shaun Jackson held me accountable as a teacher by demanding to know WHY I was asking him to do a particular assignment and always—but only—accepting a good explanation. May your memories continue to be blessings for all who knew you, as they are for me.

Introduction

Special education and juvenile justice have complex, interrelated histories in the United States. Both institutions aim to fix supposed deficits within particular kids through isolation and treatment. Although special education isn't supposed to be a punishment, it is often viewed as an undesirable system to learn and teach within. For example, laws requiring students to be placed in the general education classroom as much as possible suggest that it's better to learn with peers who don't have disabilities and that kids with disabilities have less to offer than their peers without disabilities. Special education has also had a difficult time recruiting and retaining teachers since its inception.

One current manifestation of the relationship between special education and juvenile justice is the school-to-prison pipeline (STPP). Although the full relationship between schools and the criminal justice system is complex and multidirectional, the pipeline metaphor focuses specifically on those school policies and practices that move kids in one particular direction: from schools to prison. While schools cannot solve all problems in society, nor all problems with the American justice system, we can certainly expect schools not to make things worse for the students who attend them. The STPP describes the specific ways in which schools increase the likelihood that some kids will have a negative outcome—getting arrested, and winding up in prison. These school-level factors that predict arrest can be altered by policy makers and educators.

The purpose of this book is to take a closer look at how the STPP functions for students receiving special education services. A better understanding of schools' specific contributions to kids getting arrested will help policy makers and educators to divert or block the pipeline. This book draws upon Disability Studies (DS) as a guiding framework for understanding the STPP. Most existing research on the STPP looks at student-level risk factors for arrest;

1

in other words, most existing research assumes that kids' behaviors and actions adequately explain arrest rates. However, research suggests that different behaviors among kids do not fully explain different outcomes. Instead, the consequences of kids' behaviors can vary tremendously, with kids who exhibit the same behavior experiencing radically different consequences across different schools. The differential consequences that kids experience for the same behaviors are closely related to larger social inequities such as ableism, racism, heteronormativity, and other problems. DS turns the lens of analysis from students to schools. This book asks what schools can do to decrease the likelihood that their students, particularly those receiving special education services, get arrested.

In writing this book, I draw upon three sources to examine and describe the relationship between special education and the STPP: (1) existing research; (2) data from a mixed methods study I conducted on the relationship between special education and the STPP in New York City's public schools; and (3) my own experience as both a paraprofessional and special education teacher in NYC's District 75—the citywide special education district. Using these three sources allows me to move from the general to the particular and back again, as I make sense of individual experiences within a larger context, and use particular students' experiences to better understand how and why larger patterns came to be. The mixed methods study described in this book asks which school-level factors predict an increased likelihood that schools will have students with disabilities who have been arrested, then asks seven young people (ages 15–21) who have received special education services in NYC public schools and been arrested to talk about what helps and hinders them at school.

I expected to be presenting a fairly straightforward list of things that do and do not help kids at school, along with some discussion of how and why these things might be beneficial or harmful to students. However, conducting the research used in this book also took me in some unexpected directions; the conversations that I had with young people frequently caused me to reconsider how we evaluate schools, school policies, and school practices in the first place. Rather than describing ways in which school policies and practices affected them directly, these high school students evaluated their school experiences in relation to what they imagined "regular" school experiences might be—the experiences of students who were not receiving special education services. As a result, they presented complex and occasionally contradictory claims about their own schools, such as labeling certain practices as beneficial even as they described ways in which those practices seemed to have hindered their own educations. These interviews helped me understand why some practices, such as suspension, that are consistently found to be harmful to kids persist in schools. These interviews also underscored the importance of talking to kids receiving special education services about how they make sense of their time at school.

In chapter 1, I provide a brief overview of the various perspectives on educating individuals whom United States public schools do not fit, particularly students who are considered to have disabilities and/or are considered to be "delinquent," "dangerous," or otherwise "uneducable." This overview draws upon DS to critically examine how and why schools and schooling are structured to create "winners" and "losers" (Brantlinger, 2006) rather than offering equitable educational opportunities for all children and youth in the United States. I introduce the idea of dis/ability as a social construction rather than a medical fact, and consider the implications of turning a research lens toward schools rather than students. Because dis/ability intersects with other aspects of young people's identities, and ableism is related to other organizing social process in the United States, this chapter also briefly addresses ways in which special education and involvement in the justice system disproportionately affect youth who have also been minoritized along other aspects of their identities, such as race, ethnicity, and gender identity.

Chapter 2 discusses various ways in which the STPP currently manifests in U.S. public schools, focusing on the relationship between special education and the STPP. I review existing research on how school policies and practices can push students along a pipeline toward arrest, detainment, and incarceration and use to DS to offer a critique of the existing research on this topic. Specifically, although most of this existing research looks at student-level "risk factors" to explain why some children wind up receiving "special" education services and getting arrested, this chapter argues for the importance of looking at how schools can enable or disable their students through risky educational practices. A better understanding of school-level policies and practices can help policy makers and educators alter those risky policies and practices to disrupt the STPP.

Chapter 3 begins an in-depth look at (special) education and juvenile justice in New York City (NYC). NYC has some unique features, such as a citywide special education district, but also shares many commonalities with districts across the country, so many of the problems, policies and practices found in NYC are relevant to policy makers and educators in other districts. This chapter draws upon both administrative data and interviews with young people (ages 15–21) who have received special education services and been arrested in NYC to better understand how different types of schools and school-level factors intersect with the STPP. This chapter also considers how ideas about what makes a school *legitimate* affect how students, teachers, and policy makers make sense of and evaluate particular policies and practices in complex and occasionally contradictory ways.

Chapter 4 foregrounds young people's perspectives on school staff and peers. This chapter addresses ways in which students with individualized education programs (IEPs) navigate the stigma associated with special education and disability to make sense of what adults at school are supposed to do, and whether they should try to make friends with other kids with IEPs. Navigating stigma adds an additional layer of complexity to how students with IEPs make sense of and evaluate the actions of special educators and peers with IEPs.

Chapter 5 describes ways in which administrative data about the NYCDOE as a whole, and interviews about particular students' experiences, can complement each other to provide a more nuanced and complete understanding of the STPP. Administrative data can provide a big picture and help describe the scope of the STPP in NYC. On the other hand, student interviews can help explain variability and heterogeneity within large-scale data sets to help researchers, educators, and policy makers better understand how and why school policies and practices do not affect all students in the same ways. Alternatively, student interviews can begin to illuminate how and why particular school-level policies and practices have the effect that they do. In this chapter, I describe ways in which the administrative and interview data converge and diverge, as well as ways in which the results of my study do and do not align with existing research on the STPP.

Chapter 6 considers implications for both policy makers and educators who are working toward diverting the STPP. In keeping with students' insistence that schools must first and foremost be focused on academics, this chapter suggests promising educational practices that leverage diverse students' funds of knowledge to provide access to rigorous academic curriculum for all students. Because school disciplinary policies are also closely linked with the STPP, this chapter suggests ways to promote a safe, nurturing school climate for adolescents that fulfills schools' obligation to educate students. Finally, this chapter considers whether school policies that are not closely linked with academic achievement (e.g., uniform policies) are worth pursuing.

Appendix A raises some methodological issues related to conducting research for, with, and on "vulnerable" populations. Institutional review boards (IRBs) require extra protections for children under 18, individuals with disabilities, and prisoners. While well intentioned, the layers of IRB approval required to do this study were extremely time-consuming, and may discourage researchers working under time pressures, such as those working on dissertations or against a tenure clock, from fulfilling DS's mandate to involve individuals with disabilities in any research conducted for, with, and on individuals with disabilities. This appendix provides guidance for researchers planning to conduct research with and for court-involved youth with disabilities. In addition, this appendix suggests ways in which the existing IRB processes could be streamlined to make it easier to ethically involve young people in research that affects them.

Appendix B describes the quantitative and qualitative research methods used by the mixed methods study presented in chapters 3 and 4 in more detail. Specifically, this appendix describes the data set, variables, and regression methods used for the quantitative strand discussed in chapter 3. This appendix also describes how participants were recruited, where and how interviews were conducted, and how interview data were analyzed.

Appendix C presents the interview questions used.

Chapter 1

Students Whom Schools Do Not Fit

The Brief History of Common Schooling in the United States

"Don't get me wrong, the school ain't bad or nothing, just that, it's like how people look at you and stuff."—High school student reflecting on why it can be hard to be a student in a District 75 school

Although I never asked my students how they wound up in District 75 (D75, the citywide special education district in New York City), many of these high schoolers would, at some point, share a story with me that they thought explained and justified their presence in our classroom—a "special" class in a "special" school that only educated kids who had been identified as having disabilities. I was fascinated by how my students thought about D75 and their relationship to it.

Most of my students seemed to think that their placement in a D75 school was some sort of punishment for past mistakes. One sweet ninth grader explained to me that he used to be a "bad kid" who had punched a teacher in third grade, and that was that. Of course, D75—and special education in general—is not supposed to be a punishment for bad behavior. However, my students were acutely aware that their school was not a desirable type of "special," unlike the "specialized" high schools which might focus on math, science, or the arts, and which students competed to attend from all over the city. Instead, success in a "special" high school was defined by "getting out of the ed," as one ninth-grader described his long-term goals. In other words, students did not attend this "special" school by choice, but because their teachers and counselors thought that my students needed some sort of "special" support to succeed.

A clear hierarchy existed within the schools I worked at as well, based on students' specific disability classifications, or even perceived classifications. For example, the high school I taught at was divided into two sides. On one half of the building were the "alternate assessment" classes, educating students whose individualized education programs (IEPs) exempted them from taking the New York State Regents Examinations. These students would earn a certificate of completion or attendance when they left the school at age eighteen or twenty-one, but would not earn the sort of diploma required by colleges and most jobs. Informally, many adults (and students) referred to these students as "the MRs" or "mentally retarded" students (which was still an official disability classification when I began teaching). On the other side of the building were classrooms filled with "standard assessment" students who took Regents or Regents Competency Tests toward earning a traditional high school diploma or "local diploma." These students were unofficially referred to as "the EDs," or "emotionally disturbed" students. Kids across the school and within each side actually had a range of disability classifications, but students seemed to make sense of the organization of the school as requiring them to either be considered "stupid" or "bad," with "bad" being generally preferable to these adolescents. As one student who was moved into a standard assessment class explained to his buddy at lunch one day, he "used to be mentally retarded" but "now [he was] mentally disturbed and that's better."

My personal D75 origin story started when I was nineteen years old and began working as a substitute "crisis paraprofessional" for a fourteen-year-old girl. I had no idea what sort of "special" support I was supposed to offer to this student who was only a few years younger than I was. Although I met the requirements for the job—I was over 18 years old and had a few credits of college—I had no specific background in working with kids, nor did I receive any training or support. Luckily, the other paraprofessionals seemed to know what they were doing, and often informally guided me towards tasks that were better suited toward my skillset at the time, such as ferrying paperwork to the office or picking up lunches for trips, while they worked more directly with students. It worried me to know that children who were supposed to need specialized and intensive guidance were given me instead.

Over time, I went from working as a paraprofessional to becoming a certified teacher of English Language Arts, grades 7–12. The year that I got my New York State teaching license, New York City instituted a hiring freeze, with D75 being exempt due to their perennial problem with finding and keeping qualified teachers (hiring and retaining special education teachers is a national problem. See, e.g., Carver-Thomas & Darling-Hammond, 2017). Although I did not have a special education teaching license, I was able to get a job teaching science (and then ELA and social studies) at a D75 high school because they needed teachers so urgently. There were many things I loved about that job, particularly my students, whom I got to know well in our small school. Many of my colleagues were deeply committed to working with children with disabilities, and took for granted that we were a special group of educators doing a difficult job that most other people would not and could not do.

However, my students were not necessarily thriving in this small, "special" school, nor did they seem very happy to be there, receiving the "highly specialized instructional support" they supposedly needed (according to the New York City Department of Education [NYCDOE], 2019). Although our school was well-regarded within D75, it was still considered a highly undesirable place to learn and teach by students and many teachers. All students were supposed to be working toward a "less restrictive placement" in a general education classroom or school, suggesting that kids only attended our school as a last resort, when no other options were available rather than that our school was carefully selected to nurture these particular students. Further, student outcomes did not seem to support the idea that specialized attention was necessarily benefitting students—often, only one to two students graduated each year. The school also experienced the tremendous staff turnover characteristic of special education across the United States. During my second week of teaching there, a colleague congratulated me on returning. When I laughed, he explained that they had lost several teachers during the first week of school the year before.

An additional problem I was struck by was how many of my students missed days, weeks, or months of school due to being arrested, detained, or incarcerated, and by how difficult it was for them to catch up with their schoolwork when they returned. One student disappeared for most of the spring semester, returning on the day of the school science fair, having had no time to work on his project with his partner, who generously let him stand by it anyway. Many of my students seemed to have their lives turned upside down over minor mischief. For example, kids might have to miss school to go to court if they forgot their student MetroCards and decided to hop a subway turnstile rather than risk getting to school late. Having been an extremely disorganized child myself, I was glad that my teachers and parents had worked with me to find organizational strategies (e.g., make sure that I keep my paper subway/bus pass in a wallet rather than sticking it in the pocket of my jeans and then putting those jeans through the laundry). Although they certainly seemed exasperated at times when I couldn't find something important, I never got sent to prison and can't imagine that it would have helped me or society.

Over time, I began to question how we wound up with our current, dual system in which children who have and have not been identified as having disabilities are educated in separate classrooms and schools, and taught by teachers with different types of preparation and certification. I also began to question what the relationship between special education and the juvenile and adult justice systems were. Many seemed to assume that there was something different—and deficient—about my students that led them to need a "special" education and that also made them more likely to make bad decisions and become court involved. Yet my students' needs did not seem so "special," nor did their behavior seem too different from what I remembered myself or my own classmates doing when we were the same age.

For example, many of the "special" reading strategies that I learned to help my high school students also helped me tackle tricky research articles when I enrolled in a doctoral program. Nobody had ever thought to explicitly teach me many reading strategies when I was a child because I had never been labeled a "struggling reader"; nevertheless, I continue to use these reading strategies today when I am getting myself acquainted with an unfamiliar body of research or other new genres of texts. Learning these reading strategies earlier would have made me a much better studier and learner as a child, too.

Further, many of my students' "bad decisions" didn't seem any worse than the sorts of iffy problem-solving that all adolescents (and many adults) engage in. However, my students were getting into major trouble for the sorts of minor problems that many other kids received minor punishments or even constructive support for. The downside of the "special" attention that my students received came in the form of increased surveillance and increased concern that the usual kid shenanigans that my students engaged in would somehow quickly devolve into criminal behavior. Although special education was not, itself, intended to be a punishment, it did seem to lead to increased frequency and severity of disciplinary sanctions for my students for normal kid behavior, like whispering to a friend during class or arguing with a teacher about an assignment (following a national pattern in which kids with disabilities are punished more frequently and more severely than their peers without identified disabilities for similar behaviors. See, e.g., Migliarini & Annamma, 2020). As a result, it was unsurprising that my students associated special education with punishment—the links were there.

I began to wonder: If my students' needs were not, actually, so "special," and their outcomes were not particularly good, then why couldn't they attend school with their peers who were not considered to have disabilities? How did we wind up with a dual system of education in which students with and without disabilities attend school in different classrooms and school buildings in the first place? Are there alternative ways that we could organize schools?

To begin thinking about these questions in this chapter, I will first give an overview of Disability Studies (DS) in education and explain how it differs from "special education" as a way of thinking about educating kids with (and without) disabilities. I will then recount the brief history of common schooling in the United States, and how the introduction of "common" schools quickly devolved into multiple systems for educating kids rather than ever achieving the goal of educating all children in a single, common space.

Finally, I will describe some of the ways that educators have historically framed, and continue to frame, mismatches between schools and kids. Our current dual system, in which children with and without disabilities attend school in different classrooms or buildings, was never inevitable, but came about because of particular assumptions educators, researchers, and policy makers have held about the purpose of schooling and the nature of dis/ability.

Schools cannot—and should not be expected to—cure all social ills. However, at the very least, we can—and should—expect schools to not make existing problems worse than they are. This chapter explores the roots of some of the inequities that currently exist to show that our existing dual system for educating kids wasn't necessarily natural or inevitable, and to consider ways in which schools could have been—and still could be—organized differently and more inclusively.

DISABILITY STUDIES AS A GUIDING FRAMEWORK

This book draws upon DS as a framework for understanding dis/ability, schools, and the school-to-prison pipeline (STPP, which I will describe in more detail in the next chapter). DS sees disability as a social construction rather than a purely medical or biological category; physical and mental diversity and variation certainly exist, but the decision to call some forms of difference disability is based on environmental conditions, as well as social norms about what bodies should do or look like (Valle & Connor, 2011). For example, people who rely on their hands and eyes to communicate via sign language would have no trouble holding a conversation in a very noisy room, unlike people who rely primarily on voice and ears to communicate. On the other hand, the first group would have a more difficult time communicating in the dark than the second. Rather than deciding which people "have" a disability, DS provides a framework for understanding the conditions which *enable* or *disable* each of those people.

DS also asks why certain ways of doing or being become more important in how we think about people than others (Kliewer, 1998). Why do we sort and label people based on some biological characteristics (e.g., skin color or sex) but not others (e.g., height or freckle density)? One might argue that biological sex is relevant because it is related to reproduction, but height is much more relevant on a daily basis, since it affects which cabinet shelves people can reach, how comfortable they are on airplanes, and numerous other things that will happen more frequently than having a baby. Why not sort and label humans based on height ranges, then? Similarly, people might argue that "disability" is a relevant category because it refers to things that people can't do. However, the environment influences what we can and cannot do, and tends to privilege certain ways of doing over others. For example, my *in*ability to fly is not considered a *dis*ability because humans always require assistive technology, like airplanes or stairs, when we want to move vertically rather than horizontally, so we can expect these accommodations to be widely available in the built environment (even though it would be better if I could flap my arms vigorously and take myself across the Atlantic Ocean in an affordable, environmentally friendly way). On the other hand, an *in*ability to hear becomes a problem when important information is only presented auditorily—people who cannot hear cannot, unfortunately, necessarily expect assistive technology like closed captioning or accommodations like sign language interpreters. People's ability to perform particular actions (e.g., move from one place to another or communicate with a friend) are not only a function of their particular bodily configurations but also of the environment they are in. When the built environment is not set up to support and accommodate a person's *in*abilities (e.g., my inabilities to fly and use echolocation, which have not created many problems for me so far), then that person *becomes disabled.*

The built environment currently does privilege particular ways of being and doing. For example, I can expect stairs to be widely available to help me move from one level of a building to another. This assistive technology is very helpful to me since, as mentioned, I sadly cannot fly up to the fifth floor of a building but I can use my legs to carry my body up stairs. On the other hand, ramps and elevators are still not universally available for those who use wheelchairs to move their bodies from one place to another, which makes many places inaccessible to wheelchair users. There is nothing inherently worse about wheeling than walking or running—in fact, wheeling can be a much quicker way to get around than even running (compare any marathon's wheelchair division winning times with the runner division winning times). However, people who use wheelchairs become disabled when the environment is arranged in ways that exclude them from making full use of it.

Within schools, policy makers and educators often design spaces and curricula around the idea that a "normal child" will be using it (Baglieri et al., 2011). When the built environment or curriculum does not fit students, policy makers and educators often expect children to change to better fit the school rather than changing schools to better fit their students. Ideas about who and what is "normal" come from statistics, and reflect an idea that the way the numerical majority or statistical average looks and acts is the ideal way to look and act. For example, using one's hands to communicate is considered "abnormal" and, therefore, a disability, since it is not as common as using one's mouth to communicate, even though sign languages are just as sophisticated and complex as spoken languages. Similarly, if we determine that the average age for a child to master a particular skill is, say, eleven years old, a child who masters that skill at thirteen or sixteen might be considered "abnormal," "delayed," or in need of "specialized support," even if there isn't really any particular need for that child to know the skill at such a young age (since most 11-year-olds aren't living independently and supporting themselves anyway).

Special Education versus Disability Studies in Education

The education of kids who are thought to "have" disabilities is usually the responsibility of a separate system known as "special" education. Teachers who work within this system have a separate, "special" license. "Special" education might happen within the "general" (i.e., for students without disabilities) education classroom, or it might happen in separate, segregated classes, or even schools, entirely for kids with disabilities. Because this dual system has existed for longer than anyone reading this book has been alive, it may seem inevitable to educate kids with and without disabilities in different ways and even in different places. However, this dual, segregated system for kids with and without disabilities is no more inevitable than maintaining a dual system for educating kids from different racial backgrounds or genders in segregated settings and using different methods.

Educators, researchers, and policy makers disagree about whether this dual system is beneficial or harmful for students receiving special education services and/or their peers. On one side of the debate are those who believe that disability is a biological deficit located within an individual, and that the role of schools is to detect and treat that disability through scientifically produced interventions so that students can become "more typical, more normal" (Kauffman et al., 2002, p. 154). These interventions may take place in segregated settings, such as resource rooms, self-contained classrooms, or even entirely "specialized" schools. The needs of kids with disabilities are thought to be so different from the needs of kids without disabilities that it does not make sense to try to teach them together, in the same place. Proponents of separating kids with disabilities also argue that this segregation will allow for better targeting of resources which are, unfortunately, certainly limited at many schools.

DS in education offers an alternative way of thinking about educating kids with (and without) disabilities. Rather than dividing kids into "normal students" (general education) and "abnormal students" (special education) and educating each group differently, DS-oriented educators argue that diversity, including diversity of ability, is normal among humans and present in any classroom, no matter how "homogeneously" kids are grouped. As a result, all students benefit when schools are designed to be maximally accessible and when teachers use flexible curricula that students can engage with using a range of modalities and access points.

Proponents of a "special" education for some children tend to believe that the general educational curriculum is adequate and can never be designed in such a way that it will allow all students to participate and contribute meaningfully—some students will always be too different to learn with their peers (e.g., Kauffman & Badar, 2014). Proponents of special education acknowledge that it is not a perfect system, but argue that it can be solved through some relatively minor tweaks. Problems within special education, such as disproportional representation of kids from different racial, socioeconomic, gender, language, or sexual orientation categories, are framed as technical problems that can be solved with technical solutions (Kramarczuk Voulgarides et al., 2017), like more accurate screening processes.

On the other hand, DS scholars and educators believe that education needs to be fundamentally overhauled and restructured to teach diverse kids together (e.g., Baglieri et al., 2011; Valle & Connor, 2011). Rather than changing diverse kids to better fit existing schools, DS-oriented scholars and educators advocate changing schools to better accommodate the existing diversity of students who learn within them. DS questions the idea that "normal" is a neutral term reflecting an ideal description of behaviors and development that all children should be taught to emulate (Baynton, 2001), or that the statistical average always reflects the best way and pace to do things. Instead, ideas about "normal" or "ideal" ways to be are embedded in larger biases. For example, teachers I currently work with have described times when they thought a student was being disrespectful because the student did not make eye contact; one was concerned that this might be a sign of autism. However, conversations with family members have made clear that making eye contact with adults (or not) is a norm in some cultures but not others. I appreciate that these teachers were open-minded enough to reconsider their assumptions about eye contact, but there are many, many more examples of how assumptions about "normal" student behavior are not universal.

Ableism guides many assumptions and decisions about what should be taught and how. Ableism is the assumption that "able-bodied" individuals' ways of learning and demonstrating their learning is inherently the best way to learn and do (Hehir, 2002). However, many scholars have also documented that assumptions about the best way to learn and demonstrate learning at school are culturally embedded and privilege the bodies and practices of students who are White, English-dominant, middle- or upper-class, heterosexual and cisgender, and Christian or from a Christian background, as this book will discuss in more detail.

Although many critical scholars and educators have pushed back on the idea that cultural differences should be considered disability, Baynton (2001) has pointed out that those critiques still allow "real" disability to be used as an excuse for differential and discriminatory treatment. In other words, arguing that the child who fails to make eye contact for cultural reasons does not need to be sent to a separate class because that child does not really have a disability suggests that a disability would still be a good reason to segregate a student. Disability has always been, and continues to be, considered an educationally legitimate grounds for exclusion from and inequality at school even after it became illegal to exclude or segregate kids based on race, gender, religion, and other categories.

Some Notes on Terminology

Although the arguments in this book rest upon the assumption that dis/ability is a social construction, like race and gender, that assumption doesn't mean that dis/ability (or race or gender) as an idea does not have real consequences for people. When talking about *dis/ability* as an idea, I use the "/" to acknowledge that disability and ability as ideas only make sense in relation to each other, and to ideas about what humans should be able to do (Frederick & Shifrer, 2019). However, sometimes I will specifically referring to only one side of that coin; for example, disability is the more stigmatized side than ability, and some services are intended specifically for those who are perceived to have disabilities.

Because dis/ability is a social construction, it is more accurate to refer to people as being enabled or disabled by their environments than to refer to people as "having" disabilities (Reid & Knight, 2006). Nevertheless, I occasionally use the term "students with disabilities," particularly when I am citing or summarizing someone else who uses that term. "Person-first" language is also currently the preferred identification of many people (e.g., "a person with an intellectual disability" rather than "an intellectually disabled person") and it is always best to refer to people the way they want to be referred. However, some do prefer "identity-first" terminology that forefronts that particular aspect of their identities (e.g., the Autistic Self Advocacy Network, 2019, which prefers the term "autistic person" to "person with autism") and acknowledges that disability is a valued and important part of many people's identities and experiences.

In the context of schools, this book primarily talks about "students who have received special education services" or "students with IEPs" rather than "students with disabilities." These terms acknowledge that the decision to provide a particular type of educational experience is not a natural, neutral response to a particular type of body at school. This term also acknowledges controversy within special education about who "should" be labeled as "having" a disability and about whether current practices accurately "identify" disabilities. Because I approach this problem from a DS framework, I assume that there is no single correct answer to the question of who really "has" a disability. Instead, I am interested in how the act of being formally labeled as having a disability impacts students' educational experiences. However, if I am referring to another text that simply uses the term "students with disabilities," I use that term too since not every student with a disability necessarily has an IEP or receives special education services.

Finally, I will refer to students or young people "who have been arrested" or, more broadly, to students who are "court involved." Children can become "court involved" without being arrested—for example, children in foster care have courts overseeing their placements. However, in this book, the term "court involved" is used exclusively to refer to being arrested, being on probation, attending an alternative to detention program, being incarcerated, or otherwise affiliated with the juvenile or adult justice systems, specifically.

THE BRIEF HISTORY OF COMMON SCHOOLING IN THE UNITED STATES

The introduction of common, compulsory schooling during the nineteenth century was originally based on the belief that all children should learn "a common political and social ideology" (Osgood, 1997, p. 376) together, in the same space. Although this vision of education was intended to be egalitarian, providing access to school for all children, regardless of their backgrounds, it meant that schools served a normalizing function as well as an academic one. Children were expected to conform to the political and social norms of the White, Protestant, male, English-speaking, heterosexual, middle- and upper-class, able-bodied individuals who determined the curriculum. Schools attempted to eradicate any cultural, linguistic, religious, or other diversity among students. For example, one early twentieth-century sociologist argued that a "gain" of common schooling was the "substitution of the teacher for the parent as the model upon which the child forms itself" (Ross, 1901, as cited in Kliebard, 1987, p. 93). In this way, schools could be used to try to alter the behaviors of children whose home cultures differed from dominant cultural norms, and to assimilate those children into the dominant culture.

Despite the promise of schooling for all, educators and policy makers looked to find ways to segregate or exclude some children whom schools did not seem to fit almost immediately after the introduction of common, compulsory schooling (Deschennes et al., 2001). Some children whose bodies and behaviors differed too much from the idealized norm were quickly shifted into parallel, segregated classrooms and schools that frequently had less academically oriented curricula, less qualified teachers, and fewer resources (Tyack, 1974). Many children whom schools did not seem to fit were sorted into separate institutions for the delinquent or disabled that did not even pretend to prepare children academically (Richardson, 1994). Until 1975, children could legally be excluded from school entirely if they were considered uneducable due to disability.

Part of the stated reason for segregated educational spaces has always been to provide a special, compensatory education for children who were considered too different (and deficient) to benefit from the common curriculum (Osgood, 1997). For example, the Board of Supervisors in Boston argued in 1887 that children were sent to segregated spaces "as a favor, not as a punishment." However, in the same document, the Board acknowledged that the separate classes "have never been popular either with teachers or pupils" (as cited in Osgood, 1997, pp. 391–392). It is also telling that the Board of Supervisors felt the need to say that special classes were not supposed to be "a punishment"—kids and adults were apparently making that link back then, too.

Common schooling was instituted at the same time the American eugenics movement was gaining steam, and similar ideas undergird both. The nineteenth century eugenics movement assumed that biology explained all social problems, such as poverty (Snyder & Mitchell, 2006). Rather than looking at how social conditions might create and perpetuate inequality, eugenicists blamed particular individuals' bodies for their failure to behave in ways considered normal, and therefore desirable. One strategy for fixing social problems, like poverty, was isolating particular individuals who were affected by the problem in order to keep the problem from spreading. Individuals who were considered "defective" were placed into institutions, such as hospitals or special schools, where the rest of the population could be protected from them, and where specialized professionals would ideally solve the problems in their bodies that supposedly created their abnormalities.

During the early twentieth century, educators and policy makers began arguing that schools should be organized around scientific and psychological principles rather than a common social and political ideology. Rather than gathering all students in the same place to teach them the same common curriculum, the purpose of schools shifted to teaching different kids in different ways, according to their supposed unique needs and strengths. Educators and policy makers argued that it would be more "efficient" to teach sort kids into different spaces and use different curricula for different students (Kliebard, 1987).

Educators believed that "scientific," quantitative tests, such as IQ tests, were politically neutral and could accurately measure children's intelligence and aptitude; as a result, those tests should be used to determine which children were worthy of which types of education. For example, students who scored low on psychometric tests might be excluded from participation in an academic curriculum; instead, those students might be given a vocational curriculum. Educators and policy makers assumed that many children simply were not capable of learning much. Identifying and sorting children who might or might not benefit from a rigorous education became an important function of schools (Kliebard, 1987; Tyack, 1974). However, the inherent cultural biases in these sorting tools were ignored.

The practice of identifying some students as "special" or "delinquent" and then educating them separately from their peers is neither neutral not inevitable; it has always been linked to ideas about what a "normal," "American" schoolchild should look like and do, and to assumptions about what the goals and purpose of school should be. When people assume that the goal of schools is to produce a single type of student and graduate, then all school practices will lead toward that goal. Further, valuing sameness over diversity leads to the assumption that a "good" class is one in which all kids are doing the same thing at the same time (e.g., reading the same chapter of the same book on the same day). If certain kids are doing different things, or moving at a different pace, they might be put into a different class with other kids who are doing those other things at that other pace. This process is also known as "tracking," and extensive research suggests that it harms kids who are placed in lower tracks with no benefit to kids who are placed in higher tracks (when outcomes are compared with de-tracked or untracked schools. See, e.g., Oakes, 2005; Rubin, 2003 or the position statements of many professional organizations, such as the National Association of Secondary School Principals, 2006).

Other goals for education would, of course, have led and lead to different practices and to different assumptions about what constitutes a "good" class. For example, schools might aim to identify and nurture each student's unique capabilities rather than trying to normalize and equalize students' functioning in the classroom (e.g., Terzi, 2007). With that goal in mind, an ideal classroom might be one in which each student is able to both contribute to and benefit from the class. Diversity, then, could be genuinely celebrated, and used to promote learning for all students, instead of being viewed primarily as a threat to efficiency.

LOCATING CURRENT EDUCATIONAL PROBLEMS: BODIES, COMMUNITIES, SOCIETY

Although many people agree that education in the United States does not currently lead to equal outcomes for all students, there is widespread disagreement about the nature and origin of existing problems. During the middle of the twentieth century, the assumption that all children who struggled in school did so because of their defective bodies was challenged by some educators and policy makers, who became concerned that some students were failing because they were not being given equal opportunities to be success-ful. However, while these educators and policy makers began looking for problems beyond the body of an individual student, they frequently blamed that student's family and community rather than the structures and actions of schools and society at large. For example, many educators and policy makers believed that some children were hindered by a "culture of poverty" (Spring, 1989, p. 140) or supposed cultural deficits (Gay, 2010; Ladson-Billings, 1995). The purpose of schools became providing a compensatory education to help these children overcome these disadvantages and "begin the social race at the same starting line" (Spring, 1989, p. 123) by enculturating students into dominant cultural values and norms.

Educators and policy makers who held these beliefs still expected all chil-dren to conform to school norms that reflected White, Protestant, English-speaking, heterosexual, middle- and upper-class ways of being, and believed that schools should assimilate students into these norms (Kumashiro, 2001; Utley et al., 2002). As a result, research into the problem of mismatch between schools and children frequently focused on identifying and altering supposed deficits within students' families, and communities rather than on ways in which schools could better build upon the funds of knowledge within students, families, and communities.

More recently, scholars have argued that children's communities and cultures are not the problem; schools' failures to provide culturally relevant, responsive, and sustaining curricula (e.g., Gay, 2010; Ladson-Billings, 1995, 2014; Paris & Alim, 2014) and to distribute resources in an equitable way leads to inequitable outcomes among students from different backgrounds. Educators and researchers within and outside of DS have also begun taking a more assets-based perspective toward diversity and towards all students, rejecting the "subtractive" (Valenzuela, 1999) educational practices that have traditionally sought to remove any student behaviors or characteristics that do not align with dominant cultural norms. However, even within assets-based approaches toward teaching diverse students that build upon kids' cultural and linguistic resources, many educators continue to draw a line at fully inclusive schools and classrooms for kids with diverse abilities.

I do not mean to paint an overly rosy picture of the progress that has been made toward providing equitable educational opportunities for all students. There have always been educators who are committed to building upon the strengths and funds of knowledge of all students; there certainly remain many policies and practices that blame students and families for the failures of schools. Scholars have argued that many existing educational policies and practices deliberately maintain existing inequities (see, e.g., the volume on the STPP edited by Fasching-Varner et al., 2017) and allow those who have been historically been given more educational opportunities to hoard them (Hanselman & Fiel, 2017; Lyken-Segosebe & Hinz, 2015). Special education has been one institution that, intentionally or not, has helped maintain a range of inequalities, as the rest of this chapter explores further.

DIS/ABILITY AND INTERSECTIONALITY

Disability has persistently been, and continues to be, considered a legitimate justification for inequitable treatment at, or even exclusion from school (Baynton, 2001). In addition, other groups, such girls, immigrants, religious minorities, children who are not White, and lesbian, gay, bisexual, or transgender individuals have also been excluded on the basis that their group affiliation was a form of disability. For example, girls and women were regularly excluded from many academic settings due to their supposed physical, emotional, and intellectual deficits in comparison to men (Bissell Brown, 1990). Any deviations from the male norm were considered deficits and therefore disabilities, and formed the rationale for excluding girls' participation in certain forms of education (Tyack & Hansot, 1992). One strategy that oppressed groups have taken to achieve equality has been arguing that they are not truly disabled; while it's certainly true that race and gender are not disabilities, this strategy suggests that it's okay to continue to segregate those who do "really" do have disabilities (Baynton, 2001).

Researchers have found that children continue to be differentially selected into segregated settings on the basis of their race, ethnicity, gender, and social class in addition to their disability labels. For example, Black male students are much more likely to receive their education in segregated settings for the majority of the school day than their White male or female peers, including those with the same disability labels (Blanchett, 2006), while Black girls are much more likely to be excluded from school through suspensions and expulsions than their White female peers who behave similarly (Annamma, 2018). Groups have often fought their classification as "disabled" without challenging the assumption that disability is a legitimate basis for inequitable treatment, including segregation, at school. Disproportionality is frequently challenged on the grounds that too many children who do not have "real" disabilities are currently receiving special education services; however, these arguments rest on the assumption that some children do "have" disabilities that would justify unequal treatment.

The intersection of race and disability is clearly visible in many of New York State's special education classrooms, where students from racial and linguistic minority groups continue to be overrepresented across the state (New York State Education Department [NYSED], 2015). Young people are even segregated within special education programs; Sleeter (1986) has documented how the creation of a "learning disabled" category was one way to separate White children who were struggling in school with children of color who would be more likely to be labeled "MR" or "ED." In this way, special education classes could be separated not on the illegal basis of race but based on a child's disability classification, although the end results were similar in their effect on racial segregation. Currently, students from different racial groups continue to be classified at different rates and receive different classifications, with Black students continuing to be overrepresented among those labeled as having intellectual disabilities or emotional and behavior disorders (Togut, 2011).

Tools, such as IQ tests, that test culturally specific knowledge and tend to favor privileged groups were and continue to be used to identify disability (Togut, 2011). These supposedly neutral tools have historically been and continue to be used to justify the continued segregation and exclusion of certain children from the general educational environment. For example, at one point during the early twentieth century, all the Black schools in one Georgia county were closed because "feeblemindedness was so prevalent among African American children" (Snyder & Mitchell, 2006, p. 88) when IQ tests were administered. Rather than looking critically at how the test was designed and administered to come to the unlikely conclusion that an entire group of people was flawed, educators and policy makers were comfortable locating the problem within members of a particular racial group. Culturally irrelevant formal and informal assessments continue to be used to overly select students who are not White, middle-class, and American-born into lower-track classes (Oakes, 2005) and special educational settings (Annamma, 2018).

Because disability is considered a problem waiting to be discovered within a child, children's educational environments are often not taken into account when students are being referred to special education programs (Harry & Klingner, 2006). Children who are not White or middle class, and who are more likely to be receiving inadequate general education services from inexperienced, underqualified teachers, are less likely to experience success at school according to traditional definitions and measures. These unequal educational opportunities contribute, of course, to unequal outcomes. However, blaming the child absolves educators and policy makers of any responsibility for equalizing educational opportunity.

DISCUSSION

Throughout the history of education in the United States, mismatches between school and students have been blamed on young people, their families, and their communities. However, school-level factors also impact student outcomes, such as special education placement and arrest. Although schools are not the only influence in young people's lives, school policies and practices are within the control of education policy makers and educators. At the very least, these policies and practices should not exacerbate existing social inequities. The remainder of this book explores ways in which schools continue to enable and disable children, using New York City public schools as a specific illustration.

Chapter 2

The School-to-Prison Pipeline and Dis/ability Today

"I think I just don't choose, uh, choose, like, choose my battles. I just talk, talk, talk, talk . . . I'm just trying to get my point across. [long pause] 'Cause sometimes . . . you can't get your point across. So, you have to keep, keep, keep talking to get it across."—High school student explaining why they sometimes have conflict with teachers at school[1]

Young people who have received special education services in the United States are vastly overrepresented in juvenile and adult criminal justice systems relative to their numbers in the general population (Welsh & Little, 2018); researchers have estimated that up to 85 percent of incarcerated children in this country have received or would be eligible to receive special education services (National Council on Disability, 2018). The overrepresentation of children receiving special education services in the juvenile and adult justice systems seems like an unfortunate but unavoidable problem to many people, who assume that some kids have unique problems and deficits that require a "special" education and that also lead these young people to engage in criminal behavior. Many people also assume that there is a clear and direct relationship between breaking the law and legal sanctions. However, the relationship between a child's actions and the consequences of those actions is not clear or linear; different kids experience radically different consequences for the same behaviors. For example, if two kids both break the law by using an illegal drug, one might get grounded by parents while the other might get arrested—two very different responses to the exact same behavior.

This chapter will explore some reasons why schools and the justice system respond differently to the same behaviors from different kids, focusing particular on how the idea of "risk" has shaped both education and criminal justice systems. I then turn the lens to schools, describing some school-level policies and practices that may pose risk to students, particularly risk of court involvement.

HOW SCHOOLS RESPOND TO AND SHAPE BEHAVIOR

Schools and school staff both respond to and impact the behavior of the children and adolescents within their care. Although many districts, schools, and classrooms have formal rules and policies, those rules and policies are often applied unevenly to different students and different groups of students. For example, a large study of almost one million middle and high school students in Texas found significant differences in the suspension and expulsion rates across schools "that had similar student populations and were alike in other important regards" (Fabello et al., 2011, p. 73), suggesting that different suspension and expulsion rates were probably affected by different school policies and practices rather than simply being responses to student behavior. In other words, two kids who act the same way may have very different experiences with school discipline and/or the juvenile justice system.

In addition, the ways that schools treat kids affects kids' behavior and performance at school. Children under the age of 18 are generally considered to be in need of adult guidance and supervision under the law. Older adolescents and young adults may continue to face some restrictions (e.g., around buying alcohol or renting cars) based on assumptions that they still will not be able to make decisions and exercise sound judgment in the same ways as older adults. Because public schools primarily serve children under the age of 18, and exclusively serve kids and adolescents age 21 and under, it is worth considering ways in which schools shape and guide the moral development and behavior of the young people who are trusted to their care.

Returning to the participant who couldn't "get [their] point across" at school and, as a result, got into altercations with teachers, there are three ways to frame that problem. One is to blame the student and say that they should never challenge a teacher's authority. Within this framing, the logical response is to "fix" the child (e.g., through a behavioral intervention plan) since the child is considered to be the source of the problem. A second framing is to blame the teacher and argue that the teacher should have been more responsive and receptive to students' needs. In this framing, the solution would be to help the teacher create a better classroom environment so that students can "get [their] point across" without disrupting a lesson.

Finally, this problem might also be understood as a communication problem between two individuals (albeit with different roles and statuses)—the student reports that they can't get their point across and make themselves understood. In this framing, the solution is to address the miscommunication itself, for example, using mediation. Teaching is hard, and most teachers are doing the best they can. Rather than pointing fingers at either teachers or students, it can be helpful to think about ways to bridge the gaps and mismatches that may occur between any two humans, but that also may be particularly prevalent among people who come from different cultural backgrounds and have different assumptions about the best ways to demonstrate respect for authority or communicate that there is a problem.

Risk and Bias

One idea that educators and policy makers use to determine how to frame and respond to problems at school is *risk*. Kids who behave the same way will face different consequences for those behaviors. One reason that adults respond differently to the same behaviors in different kids has to do with implicit and explicit assumptions about risk. Risk is, fundamentally, a framework for trying to predict the future, to try to determine which events are more or less likely to occur. When adults consciously or unconsciously assess risk to determine how to respond to a child, those adults are responding to actions that have not yet occurred—and may never occur—as well as to things that the child has actually done. When decisions about punishments are made based on risk, kids are being punished for things they have not actually done rather than solely for the things they have done.

People who work in education may try to assess risk in order to make decisions about how to allocate the scarce resources that are provided to many districts and schools. For example, when children are labeled "at-risk," they might receive access to extra tutoring or counseling. However, research suggests that labeling students is also likely to lead to a variety of negative outcomes including low-expectations and decreased opportunities (Annamma et al., 2013). When a child is considered to be "at-risk," that means that adults have decided that the child is more likely to experience a negative outcome than his or her peers. If adults are expecting negative outcomes anyway, it may seem like a waste to invest a lot of time, effort or support on a particular young person. Further, when a child who is "at-risk" engages in normal, developmentally appropriate mischief, that behavior may be interpreted as being more serious or sinister since it seems to confirm adults' assumptions that the child is likely to have negative outcomes.

Risk is also a concept that has also transformed the juvenile and adult justice systems over the past few decades (Rocque & Snellings, 2018). Every decision that is made within the justice system is influenced explicitly or implicitly by risk. At every point of contact, from deciding to interact with a child in the first place (e.g., deciding to stop and frisk a particular kid on the street), to setting bail, to sentencing, to determining parole, actors within the justice system are not just reacting to what a child has already done. Instead, police officers, judges, probation officers, and others are also trying to figure out how likely it is that a child will do something (i.e., commit a crime) in the future. Incorporating risk into decision-making in the justice system means that children (and adults) are punished for crimes they have not actually committed as well as those they may already have.

There are a variety of explicit and implicit ways that risk is determined within both education and the justice system. Statistics are commonly used explicitly and intentionally to try to determine the risk, or likelihood, that a child will have a particular outcome. However, formal models that attempt to predict risk are built using datasets that reflect existing biases (Berk, 2019). For example, Black kids are more likely to be punished, and punished more harshly than their White peers even though Black kids do not misbehave more often or more seriously than their White peers (Rocque & Paternoster, 2011). As a result, existing data show Black kids as being at greater risk of receiving punishments, such as suspension or expulsion, than their White peers. However, many people incorrectly interpret this risk of harsh punishment *to* Black students as reflecting an increased amount of rule-breaking *by* Black kids. Framing the problem in this way may actually increase the risk of Black kids experiencing racism at school when adults wrongly assume that they are more likely to misbehave. Schools with predominantly Black student bodies are often placed under increased surveillance (e.g., using metal detectors, police officers, and cameras) that then lead to an increased risk that normal childhood behavior is noticed, punished, and punished harshly.

Bias also affects implicit calculations of risk (O'Neil, 2017). Existing research shows disproportional representation among students from different racial groups in a variety of subjective categories, from identification with more subjective disability labels (e.g., mild intellectual disability) to punishment for more subjective behavioral infractions (e.g., disrespect). However, research also shows that different racial groups are equally represented among more objective disability categories (e.g., blindness) and disciplinary infractions (e.g., bringing a gun to school). When educators draw upon biases and stereotypes to determine that the same behavior means different things when it comes from two kids from different racial and ethnic backgrounds, those educators are assuming that some kids pose greater risks than others.

In education, it is much more common for people to think about particular kids as *being at-risk of* doing particular things than for people to think about particular school policies and practices as being *risky to* the children who attend those schools. This chapter will, instead, shift its focus to ways in which school policies and practices might be risky to various students. Specifically, this chapter will address those risky school policies and practices that may move kids, particularly those receiving special education services, along the school-to-prison pipeline (STPP).

Risk, Dis/Ability and the STPP

Disability is often framed as being inherently risky, with the risk located within particular people's bodies. In other words, policy makers and educators often suggest that kids' innate characteristics make particular outcomes more or less likely. However, Disability Studies (DS) suggests instead that certain environmental conditions present risks to individuals. For example, a physical disability does not, by itself, present a risk that a person will not be able to access certain places. After all, if a person cannot walk, there are many other options that a person could use to get around, such as using a wheelchair. On the other hand, environmental conditions, like stairs, ensure that some places are not accessible to everyone. DS turns the lens away from individual students and toward the school policies and practices that enable or disable those students. The STPP, then, is fundamentally about risky school practices that increase the likelihood that kids will wind up in prisons or jails. Looking at school policies and practices doesn't mean that kids' actions and behaviors don't matter at all, but it does acknowledge that students' actions and behaviors alone are insufficient to explain the differential outcomes that kids experience.

Current ideas about managing the risks that are assumed to be associated with disability have grown out of eugenics, described further in the previous chapter. Eugenics also attempted to be a "*predictive* discourse in that its primary impetus was the anticipatory identification of aberrancies that should be eradicated from the face of the Earth" (Snyder & Mitchell, 2006, p. 71). One way to manage risk has historically been, and continues to be, through isolating and containing people. People with disabilities, in particular, have experienced isolation and containment in institutions such as asylums or hospitals, and continue to be incarcerated in prisons at higher rates than people without disabilities (Appleman, 2018). "Risk" is perceived to be contagious, with kids who are considered to be "at-risk" also considered risky—able to infect other kids through, for example, being a "bad influence" or by disrupting instruction. As a result, kids who are considered to be at risk/risky might be quarantined in a self-contained special education classroom or juvenile facilities for the perceived protection of other children.

Schools pose higher risks for kids with individualized education programs (IEPs) than for their peers without IEPs. On average, students with IEPs are 2.9 times more likely to be arrested than their peers without IEPs; in some states, that number rises to ten times as likely (American Civil Liberties Union [ACLU], 2019). These large discrepancies among districts and states suggests that different policies and practices are differentially risky to different kids since it is extremely unlikely that kids with IEPs in different states have such radically different rates of delinquent or criminal behavior from each other, even if we were willing to accept the assumption that kids with IEPs are so much more likely to engage in delinquent or criminal behavior than their peers without IEPs.

For example, students who are classified as having a learning disability (LD) are disproportionately overrepresented at every stage in the juvenile and adult justice systems. As the largest group of kids with IEPs (33.6 percent of disability classifications during the 2017–2018 school year according to the National Center for Education Statistics), their experiences can shed light onto how kids with IEPs are moved through the STPP. Mallett (2014) explains that two hypotheses are frequently put forward to explain the overrepresentation of kids with an LD label in the STPP: (1) the school failure hypothesis and (2) the susceptibility hypothesis. The school failure hypothesis argues that overrepresentation might be explained and initiated by problems at school. For example, students identified as having LD are also disproportionately more likely to be pushed out of school, which might then put them in situations where they are more likely to engage in delinquent behavior. The susceptibility hypothesis argues more directly that adolescents who have been identified as having LD "have cognitive, neurological, and intellectual difficulties that make them susceptible to engaging in delinquent behaviors" (p. 2). This hypothesis blames kids for having unique deficits that lead to a wide range of problems including academic difficulties and delinquent behavior.

However, research suggests that a third hypothesis is necessary to consider to help explain the overrepresentation of kids identified as having LD, and other disabilities: the differential treatment hypothesis (Mallett, 2014). A large body of research shows that kids who behave the same way do not experience the same consequences for that behavior; instead, some children are subject to increased surveillance and harsher punishments for the same behaviors as their peers. This differential treatment is not random; it mirrors the biases and inequities that are present throughout U.S. society (e.g., Migliari & Annamma, 2020; Mittleman, 2018). Existing research suggests that educators view the behaviors of kids with IEPs more negatively than children without IEPs who engage in similar behaviors (e.g., Shifrer, 2013). Punishments are not distributed evenly among kids with IEPs either—this chapter will describe factors that intersect with dis/ability in ways that increase the likelihood that a child will receive school- and justice system-administered punishment.

Specifically, this chapter focuses on school-level factors that increase the likelihood that students with IEPs will get arrested, and on differential treatment of kids with IEPs by schools. When research focuses exclusively on student characteristics or behaviors to explain student outcomes, it ignores the important role that schools play in reproducing existing power structures through sorting students into particular roles and tracks, such as the "abnormal" child in need of special educational services (e.g., Baglieri et al., 2011) or the dangerous child in need of containment through punishment and arrest. Although school practices are not the only influence on student outcomes, the STPP is a specific example of school experiences causing harm to students rather than helping them.

The pipeline metaphor used to describe the STPP suggests that school experiences don't just correlate with court involvement (e.g., as explained by the susceptibility hypothesis); some school experiences may actually cause young people to become involved with criminal justice systems. Rocque and Snellings (2018) argue that there are three possible relationships that might explain the correlations between school experiences and arrest: (1) a direct connection by which students who are disciplined at school are imprisoned; (2) an indirect connection, where school experiences lead to an intermediate step such as being pushed out of school, which leads to imprisonment through increased surveillance of youth who are not in school; (3) an inverse relationship, where involvement in the justice system leads to problems at school through missed work and increased surveillance. This book will focus primarily on direct and indirect connections between schools and the justice system—the pipeline through which some kids are moved from school to prison.

Some researchers have critiqued the use of a "pipeline" metaphor for reducing the complex social environments in which schools and students are situated (e.g., McGrew, 2016). For example, Irby (2013) has described increasingly harsh disciplinary policies developed and enacted by schools over the past twenty-five years as "net-deepening" to reflect an increase in the number of rules and severity of punishments for breaking them that "catches" more students, particularly Black students, students who identify as LGBTQ, and students receiving special education services. Nanda (2019) has similarly described school disciplinary policies as a "sticky web" of surveillance and the increased criminalization of behavior by kids of color that are likely to be treated medically when exhibited by White kids, particularly those who attend wealthier schools (a pattern also found by other researchers, such as Ramey, 2015). Annamma (2018), among others, has argued that a "school-prison nexus" better describes the complex relationships between schools and the criminal justice system, which does not just flow in one direction.

These are important and valid critiques. However, the "pipeline" metaphor can be useful precisely because it does isolate and examine the contributions of schools, school policies, and school practices to young people's involvement with criminal justice systems—it looks at movement in a particular direction along a particular pathway. Many educational problems cannot be solved by schools alone; nevertheless, educators and educational policy makers can try to use their spheres of influence to make problems better rather than worse. Although researchers and policy makers should certainly keep examining and addressing ways in which out-of-school factors affect kids' likelihood of arrest and incarceration, this book will focus on what policy makers and educators can do to make schools, specifically, less risky to students with IEPs.

The next sections explore what the STPP looks like for students receiving special education services. Building upon Harry and Fenton's (2016) call to turn analyses of "risk in schooling" to schools themselves, this section discusses both *directly risky* and *indirectly risky* school policies and practices. Once educators and policy makers understand which school-level practices and policies are risky for students, we can change those policies and practices to reduce the risk of kids moving through the STPP.

Directly Risky School Policies and Practices

Directly risky policies and practices are ones that have the potential to lead to a child getting arrested at school; the relationship between the school policy or practice and arrest is clear and unmediated.

Police in Schools

The most directly risky school policy or practice is the presence of police officers in a school, since police officers can and do arrest kids at school. The increase in police officers in public schools has led to a clear shift toward criminalizing behaviors that have traditionally been addressed by teachers and administrators with school-based penalties (Brown et al., 2020; McKenna & White, 2018; Nanda, 2019). For example, kids are now arrested when normal adolescent behavior such as cutting class to play basketball in the gym, or talking back to a teacher are framed as "trespassing" or "disorderly conduct."

There has been a tremendous increase in police officers in schools since the 1970s; currently, the majority of U.S. public schools currently have police officers on campus (Bracy, 2010; Price, 2009). Courts have generally ruled that schools and school employees act *in loco parentis* and, as a result, have leeway to engage in actions, like searching lockers or questioning students, without giving students the procedural safeguards they would otherwise be entitled to, such as requiring a search warrant or reading Miranda rights (Price, 2009). School employees' power to engage in more obtrusive interactions with students has historically been balanced by the limited scope of school punishments. For example, a principal can search a student's locker without a warrant, but the consequences of that search would be limited to something school based, such as being unable to attend a school dance. In other words, the lower threshold for schools to take action was justified because school-based punishments are less severe than criminal punishments.

However, police officers in schools occupy a legally ambiguous status; sometimes they are considered to be school employees, and sometimes not. When police officers are considered to be school employees, they do not have to follow the same rules related to searching or questioning students that police officers normally have to follow. But, unlike other school employees, police officers in schools still have the power to arrest students. Increasing their abilities to search or question students has not been balanced by a decrease in the severity of punishments available to them.

The presence of police officers in schools is particularly risky in schools where the students are predominantly not White. The ACLU (2019) has found that police were more likely to focus on school discipline and less likely to coordinate with emergency teams in the presence of a threat to the school when the student body is made up of more students of color. In other words, police in schools where the students are mostly not White are more likely to *pose* a risk to students and less likely to *protect* kids from other risks, such as bomb threats or active shooters. These biases are not unique to police officers, but are, instead, systemic and endemic to every institution in the United States as many critical race theorists have found.

Indirectly Risky School Policies and Practices

Indirectly risky policies and practices are those that correlate with an increased likelihood of arrest (when controlling for student characteristics and behaviors), although the exact relationships between these policies or practices and arrest are less clear. This section will describe several risky school policies and practices that are highly correlated with arrest and that may even cause an increased likelihood of arrest, although more research is necessary to establish causality (Bacher-Hicks et al., 2019; Wilson, 2014).

School Discipline

School disciplinary policies, particularly exclusionary policies correlate highly with arrest (New York Civil Liberties Union, 2013; Roque & Snellings, 2018). Suspensions and expulsions have increased dramatically since the passages of the Gun Free Schools Act passed in 1994, leading to an explosion in "zero-tolerance" policies—by 1997, 94 percent of U.S. public schools had enacted these disciplinary policies that mandate suspensions and expulsions for certain disciplinary infractions (Eskanazi et al., 2003). Although originally intended to reduce the risk of violence in schools, fewer than one percent of suspensions and expulsions are responses to violent or threatening behavior (Stokes, 2011).

Suspensions and expulsions increase the risk that kids will get arrested (Rocque & Snellings, 2018). School characteristics and disciplinary policies have consistently predicted the likelihood that a child will be suspended or expelled more than student characteristics, or even student behavior do (Rosenbaum, 2018). In other words, the correlation between exclusionary punishments and arrest cannot be fully explained by the hypothesis that students who are suspended or expelled and arrested engage in worse behavior than their peers who are not suspended, expelled, or arrested.

Even within schools, teachers may have vastly different rates of office disciplinary referrals, suggesting that teachers' classroom management skills and choices about responses to student behavior have a strong impact on whether and how the same students get punished. For example, one study found that two thirds of the office disciplinary referrals in a middle school came from only 25 percent of teachers (Skiba, 2002). Punishment is not simply a neutral, logical response to student behaviors; differences in student–teacher interactions lead to differences in the identification of and response to problem behaviors as well.

Students receiving special education services are more likely to have experienced suspension and expulsion than their peers who do not have IEPs (Achilles et al., 2007); research suggests that adults view students' behavior more negatively when it comes from a student with an IEP than when the same behavior comes from a student without an IEP (Shifrer, 2013). Black students are also more likely to be suspended or expelled although there is no evidence that Black students misbehave more frequently or severely than their peers (Rocque & Paternoster, 2011). Instead, research suggests that educators respond differently to different students' disciplinary infractions, particularly subjective ones like being "disrespectful," based on the perceived risk that teachers think kids pose. Ironically, this differential treatment based on dis/ability and race poses risk to kids.

High-Stakes Testing

Research suggests that high-stakes testing has many negative consequences for students and teachers. High-stakes tests are those that have significant consequences for students and teachers. For example, a high-stakes test might be one that a student has to pass in order to graduate from high school, whereas a low-stakes test is one that will not, by itself, lead to a significant consequence—a student who failed a low-stakes test but met all other graduation requirements would still be allowed to graduate. High-stakes tests also have high-stakes consequences for schools. For example, schools might gain or lose funding based on these test scores. These negative effects disproportionately affect students receiving special education services.

Connor and Ferri (2007) have found that, "disabled children are more likely to be perceived as problems" (p. 73) in high-stakes testing environments because there may be real or perceived mismatches between kids with IEPs and standardized assessments. The accountability pressures around high-stakes tests may push kids with disabilities into "alternative schools" (Nanda, 2019, p. 318) or out of school entirely since students with IEPs are often perceived to be "more expensive to educate and less likely to obtain high scores" and, therefore, a "liability" (Stern et al., 2015, p. 454). Being pushed out of school correlates with an increased likelihood of arrest.

Racism

Although existing research often uses "race" as a variable for understanding the STPP, the reality is that *racism*, not race itself, is the causal factor in unequal educational outcomes, including arrest. Although well-intentioned, research that uses "race" as a variable risks reinforcing stereotypes that differential outcomes can be explained by differences among people from different racial and ethnic backgrounds. Instead, kids (and adults) from all racial and ethnic groups engage in delinquent or criminal behavior, but face very different legal consequences for that behavior (Hirschfield, 2018). Negative, differential treatment based solely on race is, of course, racism.

Black and Indigenous students are most consistently overrepresented in the STPP in the research, with Black students being three times as likely to be arrested as White students, and Pacific Island/Native Hawaiian and Native American students being twice as likely to be arrested as their white peers (ACLU, 2019). In some states, Black students are eight times as likely to be arrested as their white peers (ACLU, 2019). Black students with IEPs are four times as likely to be incarcerated as White students with IEPs (Kim et al., 2010).

Research on Latinx students and Asian American students suggests a more complex relationship that may reflect the diversity within those groups; however, Latinx students are overrepresented in the STPP in most districts and states (ACLU, 2019) (there is, of course, great diversity among both Black and Indigenous students as well).

Research shows that students of color are, in general, "punished more harshly for the same behavior as white students" (Migliarini & Annamma, 2020, p. 9). The same behaviors are perceived as more threatening, or a greater risk to the teacher and class when exhibited by kids of color than when by White kids. Researchers have argued that culturally unresponsive disciplinary styles may lead to the overrepresentation of Black students among those who are suspended, expelled, placed in special education, and arrested (e.g., Blanchett, 2006; Gay, 2010; Ladson-Billings, 1995).

The racial composition of schools and an individual student's race affect which students are suspended, expelled, or arrested, even though students from different racial and ethnic groups appear to engage in the same rates and types of disciplinary and legal infractions. For example, one study found that Black students were 27% more likely to receive a disciplinary report than other students after taking into account a variety of student characteristics and students' conduct at school as perceived by their teachers (Rocque & Paternoster, 2011). Several studies have found that while rates of mandatory suspensions for less discretionary violations of school rules, such as bringing a gun to school are similar across all racial and ethnic groups, Black students are more likely to receive punishments for discretionary violations of school rules such as disrespect (e.g., Fabelo et al., 2011), indicating that Black students do not necessarily break rules more frequently than other students but that they are more likely to be punished.

Further, the racial composition of a school often affects which resources are made available to those schools. For example, schools run by the Bureau of Indian Education are consistently underfunded by the federal government, leading to difficulties attracting and retaining qualified teachers, guidance counselors, and other educators. Research suggests that American Indian/Alaska Native students are also disproportionately more likely to experience exclusionary discipline than their White peers, and more likely to be removed from the classroom for minor disciplinary infractions such as, ironically, violations of attendance codes (Sprague et al., 2013). This discrepancy is particularly worrisome given research suggesting that American Indian/Alaska Native kids who become court involved (e.g., arrested or detained) are more likely to experience harsher consequences at every step of the process and, as a result, less likely to be returned to school than their White peers (Hopper, 2016).

Latinx students are more likely to receive harsher punishments and treatment at every step along the STPP than their White peers, from first encounters with police to sentencing (Arya et al., 2009). Further, Latinx students are less likely to be offered rigorous, culturally relevant learning opportunities in well-resourced schools. With harsher treatment at sentencing (longer sentences and higher likelihood of being placed in adult prisons), Latinx children are also less likely to return to school after arrest than their peers.

Although research on Asian American and Pacific Islander (AAPI) youth in the justice system is sparse, with many simply being classified as "Other" in demographic reports there has been a tremendous increase in AAPI youth and adults in prison since the 1990s (Jung et al., 2015). The category AAPI aggregates data across ethnic groups with very different histories, educational experiences, and educational opportunities in the United States, with many subgroups of AAPI students being overrepresented in the STPP. One particularly worrisome consequence of the STPP for some AAPI immigrant youth in particular is increased risk of deportation among those with criminal records. Future research must address the heterogeneity within this group and the diverse experiences AAPI youth have with the STPP.

Sexism, Transphobia, and Heteronormativity

Gender and gender presentation also affect a variety of educational experiences, such as who is identified for special educational services, and who is more likely to get into trouble and for what. Boys are more likely to both receive special education services (Blanchett, 2006) and get arrested (Gage et al., 2012) than girls. However, researchers have also found that boys and girls get classified for special education services and arrested for different reasons (Blake et al., 2011; Gage et al., 2012; Sharpe & Gelsthorpe, 2009). Rigid gender expectations may lead to trouble at school when kids, particularly girls, do not conform to assumptions that girls should be more quiet and compliant than boys. For example, Sharpe and Gelsthorpe (2009) argued that girls who get into trouble in school or with the law are subject to "double condemnation" for both getting into trouble and "flouting the values of femininity" (p. 200). Within the juvenile justice system as well, girls are at greater risk of being charged for "less serious crimes than boys" (Winn & Behizadeh, 2011, p. 161). In addition, Gage et al. (2012) found that "following a conviction, girls generally appear to be punished more severely than boys" (p. 604).

Students' experiences with schooling, special education, and arrest are also affected by responses to their sexual orientation and gender presentation. Young people who are not heterosexual or cisgender may experience discrimination from school staff, security, police, and courts (Winn, 2011). Girls, in particular, are at risk of receiving harsher punishments at school when their behaviors don't align with normative ideas about femininity. For example, girls who reported same-sex attraction had 95 percent higher odds of being disciplined, but there was no higher risk for boys who reported same sex attraction; most of this discrepancy could not be explained by parent-reported behavior problems (Mittleman, 2018). The risk of harsh punishment extends to the juvenile justice system, where gay, transgender, and gender nonconforming youth, particularly gender nonconforming girls, are over-represented; this overrepresentation cannot be explained by higher rates of misbehavior (Hunt & Moodie-Mills, 2012).

Race intersects with gender identity and sexual orientation to affect the risks different kids face at school. For example, Black girls have different experiences at school from Black boys although they are the same race; they may experience neglect from adults at school who assume that girls are more mature and need less help (Crenshaw et al., 2015). Black girls are also much more likely to be punished at school and to receive more severe sentences in the juvenile justice system than girls of other races, even though they are all girls (Crenshaw et al., 2015).

Researchers have found that Black girls are punished when they fail to conform to educators' ideas about what "ladylike" behavior should be (Murphy et al., 2013, p. 590) and when educators interpret their behaviors through the prism of stereotypes around Black girls' femininity (Blake et al., 2011). Black girls are more likely to be criminalized based on their appearance (Thompson et al., 2020). One year, Black girls made up 90 percent of all girls who were expelled from NYC public schools; no White girls were expelled at all that year (Hill, 2018).

Adding dis/ability to the mix further affects the risks that kids face at school. Annamma (2018) found that one of five girls of color "with dis/abilities" were suspended during the 2013–2014 school-year (p. 22). Migliarina and Annamma (2020) noted that "disabled girls of color and queer and gender noncomforming girls of color experience higher rates of suspension than girls of color without disabilities . . . or cisgender heterosexual girls of color" (p. 9).

Other Forms of Discrimination

Research consistently shows that racism, sexism, transphobia, and heteronormativity pose risks for students with (and without) IEPs at school. However, more research is necessary to better understand the specific ways that these forms of oppression intersect to create specific problems for individual children, particularly in relation to the STPP.

Other forms of discrimination pose problems to students that are related to the conditions of the STPP, although the relationship between these forms of discrimination and the STPP have not been researched much. For example, the relationship between religious discrimination and school outcomes has not received much attention, perhaps because schools do not regularly keep data on students' religious affiliations. However, the presence of this form of discrimination in U.S. schools, as well as anecdotal evidence of ways in which this form of discrimination can lead to increased risks of kids interacting with law enforcement, suggests that this area is worth understanding better. Both Islamophobia and antisemitism are common in U.S. public schools (see, e.g., the Anti-Defamation League's ongoing research into both problems), and have many negative consequences for Muslim and Jewish youth. The lack of any representation of many other religious groups (e.g., Sikhs, Buddhists, Hindus, and others) may lead to risky conditions for children who practice or who come from families that practice those religions. For example, many Sikhs continue to be targets of anti-Muslim hate crimes, and

Sikhs who wear turbans may be perceived as threats by others, including by school staff. More research is needed to better understand the experiences of students from religious minority groups at school in general, including their experiences with the STPP.

DISCUSSION

Research suggests that schools pose risks to students, particularly students receiving special education services. These risks are mediated by other larger social problems, like racism. The STPP, then, describes school policies and practices that increase the risk, or likelihood, that children will get arrested and incarcerated. Although other factors certainly affect the likelihood that kids will become court involved, the school-level policies and practices that predict an increased likelihood of arrest can be altered education policy makers and educators to reduce the likelihood that schools will cause harm to their students. The following chapter will begin exploring how the STPP operates in NYC public schools.

NOTE

1. Because of the small number of participants in this study (seven total, only two of whom identify as girls), I use "they" as a singular, gender-neutral pronoun to refer to all participants in order to reduce the likelihood that adults who helped me recruit participants will be able to recognize particular students. For clarity, I use "themself" when referring to a singular participant and "themselves" when referring to multiple people.

Chapter 3

Special Education and the School-to-Prison Pipeline in New York City

An Overview

"It's just a school, is—even though it was, like, a District 75 . . . you leaving out of here with a lot of stuff that you're learning at other schools, regular schools."—High school student explaining why they thought their school was a good school

There are many things that make the New York City (NYC) public school system exceptional. The most notable feature is its size: with 1.1 million students attending publicly funded schools, the New York City Department of Education (NYCDOE) educates more children than there are residents of eight U.S. states and runs over 1,800 public schools. As a result, NYC is uniquely positioned to offer students many different types of schools. In theory, offering a diverse selection of schools could reduce the mismatches that may exist between a rigid, standardized school system and the students who learn in those schools.

On the other hand, efforts to create truly unique or specialized schools that cater to diverse kids' strengths and needs have been stymied by the same forces that constrain educational innovation all over the country. This chapter will first give an overview of some of the different types of public schools found in NYC, and explore the different opportunities they offer to kids with (and without) disabilities. These differential opportunities intersect with the school-to-prison pipeline (STPP) in diverse ways. Next, this chapter will address how ideas about what a legitimate, "regular" school should look like and do affect education policies and practices for kids with (and without) disabilities, as well as how we evaluate those policies and practices. Special education, in particular, is often stigmatized and, as a result, faces particular pressures to establish and maintain legitimacy. Finally, this chapter will explore which school-level factors correlate with an increased likelihood of kids with IEPs getting arrested in NYC public schools.

Throughout this chapter, I will draw upon data from a mixed methods study on the relationship between special education and arrest in NYC public schools that I conducted between 2015 and 2018 (more information about the methods I used can be found in Appendices B and C). Specifically, I used data from semistructured interviews conducted with seven young people (ages fifteen to twenty-one) who had received special education services in NYC public schools and been arrested. I also used administrative data from the NYCDOE, New York State Education Department (NYSED), and New York University Research Alliance to examine: (1) how students who have received special education services in NYC public schools and subsequently been arrested present and explain what helps and hinders them at school and (2) which school-level factors predict an increased likelihood that students with individualized education programs (IEPs) will get arrested.

NEW YORK CITY AND ITS SCHOOLS

Describing a place as vast and diverse as NYC is daunting. The numbers alone (so many people! so many languages!) suggest some of the complexity of this place, but fail to capture the lived experiences of the children, families, and teachers who live and work here. This section describes the structure of the NYC public school system in more detail, focusing on the differential opportunities that different schools offer kids with IEPs. Throughout this section, I will use quotes from the interviews I conducted to show the perspectives of some of the students with IEPs who have learned in each type of school.

Specifically, this section will address some of the more distinctive types of schools that are part of the NYCDOE and that kids with IEPs might attend: District 75 schools; District 79 schools; small schools; and charter schools. The high school students I interviewed contrasted each of these types of schools with "regular" schools, and evaluated school policies and practices in relation to these imagined "regular" schools, as I will describe further in the following section. Although the stated goal of running many different types of schools is to increase choices and options so that each student will find the best possible school for their individual needs, the reality is that not all schools accept all kids with IEPs, meaning that their choices are constrained.

Participants had attended a range of schools for middle and high school prior to getting arrested. Specifically, participants had attended "community schools," or schools that primarily educate kids without disabilities; entirely specialized schools (part of District 75, or D75 in NYC); and/or charter

Table 3.1 **Participants' Schools**

	Community Schools	D75 Schools	Charter Schools
Middle schools	3	2	0
High schools	4	1	1

schools. The number of schools in this chart adds up to more than seven because most students had attended several schools for middle and/or high school (table 3.1).

Because this study focuses on schools and school-level factors rather than on individual kids, I use issue-focused analysis rather than case-focused analysis. Issue-focused analysis looks selectively at how different participants do (or do not) address a particular topic related to the STPP (Weiss, 1994). As a result, I will describe themes that I found across participants' descriptions of schools, as well as tensions within themes—areas where participants complicated or contradicted their own or others' claims—rather than presenting cases of particular students' experiences with the STPP.

Focusing on themes rather than individual trajectories also helps preserve confidentiality, particularly local confidentiality. As described further in Appendix B, adults who knew the participants and the schools they had attended helped me recruit participants and, as a result, there is a risk that adults who know participants will be able to identify them and their schools. For example, only one participant had attended a charter school, so the adults who helped recruit this participant would easily be able to identify this student from a table of participants, even if a pseudonym was used. Because case-level analysis does not align with the goals of this study and poses a threat to participants' confidentiality, I will be masking participants' identities as much as possible throughout this book. I will present quotes related to particular themes, but only give as much context as necessary (e.g., that a particular quote referred to a D75 school if that information is relevant, but not necessarily which participant said that quote). As mentioned earlier, I also refer to all participants using the gender-neutral pronoun "they" as a singular pronoun to preserve confidentiality.

Before I return to considering participants as a group, I want to offer an example of one child's unique sense of humor to suggest the full human beings that are behind the themes and patterns presented here. While describing theater, a class this participant particularly disliked, this high school student drily told me: "We was about to do a play. But then I got caught up for a warrant, so. I'm glad I got caught up for that warrant though." Formal interviews and informal conversations were filled with astute observations, jokes, and young people's acts of kindness toward me, their peers, and other adults, sometimes in difficult settings and circumstances.

District 75 and District 79: Citywide School Districts

One particularly unusual feature within the NYC public school system is its two citywide districts—District 75 (D75) and District 79 (D79). Unlike the 32 regional districts, D75 and D79 operate schools all over the city.

D75 is the citywide special education district. All D75 schools and programs (e.g., programs in hospitals or home tutoring) educate only students with IEPs. That means that kids in D75 schools do not interact with kids without IEPs at any point during their school day—from busing, to recess, to lunch, to dismissal. Equally important, kids without IEPs and their teachers have no opportunity to interact with students in D75 programs. Although special education policy often suggests that they are the main beneficiaries of "inclusion" (educating kids with and without disabilities in the same room), kids without disabilities benefit from inclusion as well, and both groups benefit even more from truly inclusive teaching practices (which I describe in more detail in chapter 6). Further, individuals who are considered able-bodied may hold inaccurate, biased views of who attends D75 schools or what happens there, although it is outside the scope of this book to address those misconceptions in detail.

D75 offers the possibility of an extremely restrictive environment for many children receiving special education services in NYC that may not be available in other, smaller districts. The Individuals with Disabilities in Education Act (IDEA, 2004) allows for the removal of a child from general education classes and schools "if the nature or severity of the disability is such that education in regular classes with the use of supplementary aids and services cannot be achieved satisfactorily." Due to the ambiguous nature of the law, different schools, districts and states may interpret it differently; The National Council on Disability (2018) found that different states placed students with disabilities in general education settings at very different rates, noting that New York was one of the states with the highest rates of segregating students with IEPs into separate classes. The Council found that the "highly inclusive states" tended to be more rural. Although it's certainly possible that these states also have more inclusive educational philosophies, it is also possible that smaller, rural districts that may only have a single secondary school simply don't have the capacity to segregate kids with disabilities to the extent that large, urban districts like NYC do.

D75 educated 22,360 students in the 2013–2014 school year, the year which the administrative data for this study came from. Although not all children with IEPs in NYC are educated in D75, all children attending D75 schools have IEPs. Of those students, 73 percent were male, and 27 percent were female. One percent identified as American Indian or Alaska Native, 39 percent Black or African American, 39 percent Hispanic or Latino, 7 percent Asian or Native

Hawaiian/Other Pacific Islander, 14 percent White, and one percent multiracial. 22 percent were considered "Limited English Proficient Students," and 67 percent "Economically Disadvantaged," meaning they or their families received FRPL or other economic assistance programs including food stamps, the Earned Income Tax Credit, or foster care (NYSED, 2014). By comparison, the district as a whole educates fewer English Language Learners (13.2 percent), fewer Black students (25.5 percent), and more "economically disadvantaged" students (72.8 percent). Recent reforms intended to move kids from self-contained special education classes into integrated co-teaching classes that educate kids with and without IEPs, led by both a special and general education certified teacher, have not had much effect on D75.

The disproportionate overrepresentation of Black children in D75 schools mirrors a national trend in which these students are more likely to be placed in restrictive settings for reasons that the National Council on Disability (2018) tactfully referred to as "variables other than child-related factors" (p. 25). As has been addressed in previous chapters, kids from different racial and ethnic groups who behave and perform in identical ways will be given different opportunities to access more advanced curriculum; punished at different rates; and given differential access to potentially beneficial supports such as extra time on tests, or more harmful special education practices such as segregated school settings.

Although the purpose of D75 is to provide students with unique, specialized support, the students I spoke with who had attended D75 schools were suspicious of any ways in which their schools differed from imagined "regular" schools and spoke favorably about ways in which their D75 schools seemed to be similar to "regular" schools.

One student who attended a D75 school said that, if they had to give a hypothetical new student advice about being successful at their school, they would simply say, "I'd say, don't come here bro. Just don't. Even though it might help you a little bit, you just want to get out." This seemingly contradictory statement—that a specialized school "might help you a little bit" but the new student would still "just want to get out" reflects the stated goals of special education, which are to provide specialized support and then, ideally, move a student through the continuum of placements into a less restrictive one. This student understood their D75 school to be the least desirable place to be, even when the school helped them. For example, the student further clarified, "I was just suggesting, don't come to this school. But it does help you accomplish some goals and stuff, or whatnot. I can admit to that, but yeah . . . Like me. My anger, I get—it's a little bit down, but you know, it's got—uh—people say it's gotten a little bit better. I'm gonna say yeah. So you know. It helped me a little bit." Although the student acknowledged that the school had helped them "a little bit" with their anger, they still reiterated their advice to avoid the school entirely. The idea that the school primarily helped the student with a nonacademic skill rather than academic support may also have contributed to the student's negative feelings about their school, as I'll explore further in this chapter.

Another student who had a more positive experience at a D75 school still felt the need to explain that the school was like a "regular school" in the quote that opens this chapter. This student clarified: "it's just a school, is—even though it was, like, a District 75 . . . you leaving out of here with a lot of stuff that you're learning at other schools, regular schools." Rather than describing any part of the curriculum and how it had benefited them, this student expresses happiness that they have access to "stuff that you're learning at . . . regular schools." This participant implies that the curriculum at "regular" schools is the ideal curriculum, and does not question its content or delivery at their school. However, this participant explains that there is stigma associated with not being in a "regular" school, noting that, "regular ed will make fun" of students at the D75 school. However, this participant argues that this stigma is misplaced because the D75 school is more similar to a "regular" school than other "regular ed" students realize, explaining, "they don't know that we learning the same thing that they do." This argument rests on the assumption that differences between D75 and "regular" schools reflect poorly on D75 schools, while similarities reflect favorably on D75 schools.

Participants who had attended D75 schools, in particular, expressed wariness for any policies and practices that seemed to deviate from "regular" school policies and practices that they imagined occurred in non-D75 schools. These participants described a hierarchy of schools, with D75 schools on the bottom and "regular" schools on top, mirroring the assumption that the "least restrictive," or most like general education, placement is the best. For example, two participants explained that they had wound up at D75 schools because they had been "kicked out" of other schools, suggesting that D75 schools are the places where excluded and discarded students are sent. Participants' descriptions of this hierarchy reflects a common understanding that "less restrictive" settings (i.e., those with fewer students with IEPs) are more desirable than more restrictive settings and that students in less restrictive settings (i.e., students without IEPs) are also more desirable students. For example, a recent study on special education in the NYCDOE asked, "Is Special Education Improving?" and used "integration" with general education students through placement in less restrictive settings as one of the key measures for addressing that question (Stiefel et al., 2017). The close alignment between how participants described "good"/"regular" versus schools that educate students receiving special education services in particular, and how policymakers and many practitioners describe the most and least desirable settings for educating students with IEPs, suggests that participants in this study have internalized the hierarchies reflected in how NYCDOE schools are structured and organized.

D79 is the citywide "Alternative Schools District," which runs a range of schools and programs, including the schools that educate kids who have been arrested and are detained or placed in juvenile or adult facilities within NYC (e.g., East River Academy on Rikers Island and Passages Academy schools for kids in nonsecure or limited secure facilities). Some of these schools were created or expanded after the Close to Home Initiative, written into the 2012–2013 New York State budget, encouraged NYC to keep kids within the city after arrest rather than sending them upstate, where it is difficult for families to maintain contact (Office of Children and Family Services [OCFS], 2015). D79 also runs other schools and programs, such as "transfer high schools" which serve older high school students (ages sixteen to twenty-one) who have been unsuccessful at other schools; alternative learning centers for kids who are suspended; and adult learning programs such as preparation for the high school equivalency examination.

The high school students I spoke with also looked at D79 schools unfavorably. When I asked one participant what they liked least about their school, they responded that, "It was, like, in a bad area," then clarified, "It was next to a suspension school . . . it was, like, fights that happened." This participant acknowledged that they had been suspended from school several times, but differentiated themself from the students at the alternative "suspension school," explaining, "Everybody was cool with me, cause even when I was like, bad and I got suspended, they were cool with me because they knew I wasn't, like, the type of kids to just start trouble or something. Like, why you up here? you know you not supposed to be here. We don't see you fighting like that. You're just the funny kid, the class clown." This high school student differentiates between getting suspended occasionally ("I probably only got suspended probably like five times") and actually being a particular "type of kid"—"the type of kids to just start trouble." Attending a suspension school signaled a qualitative as well as quantitative difference between the students at the D79 school and this participant.

Small Schools and "School Choice"

Mayor Michael Bloomberg took control of the public school system in 2002 and initiated a range of changes to respond to the problem of mismatch between schools and students. He named his plan "Children First" and argued that it would deliver "bold" changes to education in NYC because "incremental changes . . . will not deliver the results that the public has a right to expect and our parents have a right to demand" (NYCDOE, 2009). However, as I will discuss later in the chapter, it is not always easy to make significant changes to institutions. Research suggests that changes that did occur in NYC schools have not necessarily benefited kids receiving special education services (among other groups).

Bloomberg took control of the NYCDOE shortly after the passage of No Child Left Behind (2001), which required schools to maintain "adequate yearly progress" on standardized tests or be closed down. The majority of large, older schools in NYC have closed down as a result of NCLB and, under Bloomberg, were replaced with smaller schools. These small schools were intended to provide more personalized support for students. The NYCDOE also replaced many zoned middle and high schools with specialized high schools (e.g., focusing on the environment or journalism) that students needed to apply to attend. This initiative has had numerous problems, including an exacerbation of racial segregation within the NYC public school system. Small schools also frequently don't have the resources required by IEPs and, as a result, some have refused to accept many students with IEPs. The Office of Civil Rights filed a discrimination complaint about small schools not educating enough students with IEPs in 2007.

Although small schools are intended to be nurturing places for adolescent students, participants described some ambivalence about attending small schools, noting that it could be difficult to avoid other kids who pushed their buttons, and that small schools could not offer as many opportunities as larger ones. For example, one participant described their small, co-located school as being different from other schools because: "this school much more smaller. And, I don't know about downstairs and upstairs, but, I know this is small. Being stuck around here, yeah. It's small." This participant felt "stuck" in a small space rather than nurtured within a smaller community. Another participant compared two schools they had attended saying that the larger one was "better . . . It was more, it was different—it was a lot of different stuff there. And [the smaller one]—the one I go to now, is like, not a lot of people there." Having a very small group of classmates, in this student's case, made it difficult to find compatible friends or to get breaks from other students when they might be experiencing some disagreements over the course of the day.

Another important consequence of "school choice" has been that NYC students increasingly attend schools outside of their neighborhood for middle and high school. As a result, students are not necessarily beginning middle school with any of the friends they have made in their neighborhoods or elementary schools. One high school student I spoke with contrasted time at a zoned school with time at a small, unzoned school saying that the community school was "fun" and "lit" because it "had a lot of people I knew" from their neighborhood. However, when they transferred to a small school, they "just never went" because they "coulda made friends" but did not. This participant explained that kids in the newer school were "not from where I'm from. They were just different . . . I can't explain it. They was just different." Not having friends from the neighborhood contributed to school being an unappealing place for this participant, and hindered this student's academic success.

On the other hand, some participants did find attending a small school to be beneficial. One participant explained that they liked the most recent school they attended because it had, "less kids . . . Like, when you in a bigger school, they don't really—I feel like they don't really care about your education . . . like, some teachers probably do. But. When there's more than over 20 something kids in a class, they don't really care. Cause, you got one being disrespectful. They got one that wanna learn, but they can't learn 'cause everybody else wanna act crazy . . . they really take the time out here, like, to help us." This participant's reflection that the small school allowed teachers to "really take the time" better reflects the intent of small schools. However, the diverse perspectives suggests that small schools aren't necessarily magic, and may create unique challenges that students need to learn how to navigate.

Charter Schools and "School Choice"

There are 260 charter schools within NYC, which are overseen by the NYCDOE or New York State. These schools educate over 125,000 students. On average, charter schools enroll a slightly smaller percent of students with disabilities than the city as a whole (18.1% versus 19.5% in 2019). However, this aggregation of students with disabilities across all charter schools can be misleading since some charter schools are exclusively for kids with IEPs (e.g., the NYC Autism Charter School network) and, as a result, serve as additional options for restrictive settings. Further, charter schools do not necessarily educate students with all disability labels or offer a full range of class sizes, accommodations, and other services to be truly accessible to all. When data from these schools that are entirely filled with kids with IEPs are averaged with data from other charter schools, it is clear that many charter schools are not meeting their obligations as publicly funded schools to educate students with disabilities (Stern et al., 2015).

Some charter schools in NYC advertise different supports, structures, and/ or curriculum from other local schools. For example, charter schools might offer extended school days or multiple languages other than English to study. However, the students I spoke with did not necessarily find these features helpful and, in some places, described them as being harmful.

For example, one participant spoke enthusiastically about how "fun" one charter high school was because it offered "a lot of different classes." However, that same student also said that they had not taken any of those special classes, and also admitted that they did actually not regularly attend that "fun" school. This participant seemed to like the idea that the school had a variety of course offerings even though the special courses had not benefited the student directly. This participant blamed themself for failing to attend this "fun" school, mirroring a common assumption that truancy results from student' flaws rather than school practices (e.g., Rocque et al., 2017). However, research suggests that school practices, such as teachers' classroom management techniques, make it more or less likely that students will attend school (e.g., Havik et al., 2015). Later in the interview, this participant described how the school's extended day was simply too long—the participant wound up leaving school at lunch each day and, as a result, failed many afternoon classes.

As this section suggests, the promise of offering different types of schools to meet the needs of diverse children is not always realized, and schools don't always function as they are intended to. Complicating matters further, participants' evaluations of their schools were mediated by ideas about *legitimacy*—what people think schools are supposed to look like and do—as much as by how school policies and practices actually help or hinder students.

"REGULAR" SCHOOLS AND SPECIAL SCHOOLS: WHAT MAKES A SCHOOL LEGITIMATE?

Throughout the interviews I conducted with young people, I noticed disconnects between their overall assessment of a particular school policy or practice (e.g., as "fair") and their description of how that policy or practice actually affected them (e.g., negatively, by causing them to feel alienated from school). This complex and occasionally contradictory relationship between how kids assessed particular practices and how they and existing research suggest those practices actually affect kids can be explained, in part, by ideas about what a legitimate "regular" school is supposed to look like and do.

Five of the seven participants introduced the idea of "regular" schools as an imagined and ideal setting for students. The students I spoke with would evaluate their school's policies and practices in relation to whether those policies and practices were similar to what they imagined happened at "regular" schools. For example, when I asked students what they would like to change about the schools they had attended, one student told me that they wished their special education high school were more "like a regular school." When I asked what would make their school more "regular," the student suggested adding "ninth period classes, we don't have that . . . We ain't that type of school." I asked which additional classes this student wished they could take, and the student replied simply, "Any classes that we don't have ninth period. [laughs] Yup." This student did not have any particular classes in mind, nor did they offer an academic or practical justification for this desire (e.g., that taking more classes would help them learn more or make them a more competitive applicant for college). Instead, the rationale was simply that "regular" schools offered more options, but their school, unfortunately, was not "that type of school."

Decisions about public education are made not only based on research on "what works" but also on key stakeholders' ideas about what schools are supposed to look like and do. Tyack and Cuban (1995) refer to the durable structure of U.S. public schools and their resistance to change as the "grammar of schooling." They argue that many educational innovations, such as ungraded classrooms or project-based (rather than subject-specific) classes have failed because they did not conform to people's ideas of what schools are supposed to look like or do. It's not enough for research to suggest that a new approach, practice, or structure might benefit kids. Parents, voters, and students themselves might think that the new way of doing things is simply too far outside of the parameters of what a school is supposed to look like and do, preferring subtle changes to bolder ones.

The idea that any new approaches to education need to work within the rules of an existing grammar of schooling connect to larger ideas about how institutions gain legitimacy in general. Policy makers and educators must ensure that schools remain legitimate institutions in the eyes of key stakeholders such as voters, parents, and students. Education, in general, is a field that suffers from low prestige, and special education is often looked down upon even within the field of education. As a result, policy makers and educators often try to maintain the legitimacy of special education as an institution through its proximity to two higher status fields: medicine and general education. Special education is structured and described in ways that align with the norms of each of these professions. When special education does things differently from either of those two professions, its legitimacy is challenged, even if there are sound educational reasons for the field to do so.

Thinking about dis/ability primarily through the lens of medicine works as both a framework for trying to understand what dis/ability is and also as a means of imbuing authority, prestige, and legitimacy to educators who work with kids with disabilities in particular and to special education in general. In this paradigm, special educators are analogous to medical specialists who, according to Fuchs et al. (2014) provide "intensive care" (p. 14) using "intensive interventions" (p. 17) that cannot be achieved in the general education setting, which is analogous to "primary care" medicine (p. 14). Kauffman et al. (2016) argue bluntly that special education won't be "taken seriously" (p. 11) unless it follows other fields' "advances" and "its labels become more specific, not more general" (p. 5). In other words, "special" education is staffed by "special" educators who supposedly have more or better knowledge than "general" educators. However, others have argued that medicine as a field has limited utility for special educators beyond its perceived legitimacy, claiming that, "The language of traditional special education is saturated with medical terminology that imbues it with the authority of pseudo-science" (Connor, 2013, p. 497).

Within education, general education is frequently held up as the ideal—or at least mostly good—model of education that special education should emulate as closely as possible, and that students receiving special education services should aspire to be as close to as possible. For example, students with IEPs are supposed to be educated in the "least restrictive environment" under the law, which positions general education as the most desirable place and curriculum for any student. There is an assumption that the general education classroom is already doing things well, so any mismatches between class and student are the fault of the child with the IEP. Special education curriculum is also supposed to be aligned with the general education curriculum as much as possible. For example, the New York State Alternate Assessment for kids who do not take standardized tests uses Alternate Grade Level Indicators that are "clearly related to the grade-level content," with the NYSED explaining, "While the content is reduced in scope and complexity, students with significant cognitive disabilities are held to high expectations in order to achieve the New York State learning standards" and "experience a richer learning experience." The expectation is that special educators and students with IEPs will adapt to the general education curriculum, but that general education does not have anything to learn from special education.

When I first started working as a paraprofessional, students in D75 often participated in a "functional" or "daily living" curriculum that focused on things like doing laundry or making peanut butter sandwiches. Restricting the curriculum to "daily living" activities rather than "academic grade level indicators" probably unnecessarily limited many students' options. For example, Jamie Burke, a seventeen-year-old student with autism, argued, "it was so foolish to ask me to learn to tie my shoes"—a process that he had to work on at school until he finally learned at age fifteen—instead of focusing on other things that were more important and interesting to him, like speaking or learning Shakespeare (Biklen & Burke, 2006, p. 171). However, there is no reason that "functional" or "practical" skills have to be limited to basic tasks like shoe tying or sandwich making. As a high school student, I learned calculus but nothing about finance—calculus is considered a legitimate subject for schools to teach, while financial literacy is often offered as a consolation prize to students who are considered incapable of learning calculus. Yet, people get graduate degrees in finance—surely it could be taught to high school students in complex, rigorous ways. As an adult, I have very little use for calculus, even as a researcher who uses statistical analyses. However, I regularly wish I had more background in "functional" tasks like doing my taxes or figuring out my retirement plan. General education might benefit from more "functional" education as much as special education might benefit from more "academic" education. However, the perceived illegitimacy of special education makes it unlikely that general education borrows ideas from special education.

"IT'S JUST NOT THE SCHOOL'S BUSINESS": STUDENTS' PERCEPTIONS OF WHAT "REGULAR" SCHOOLS DO

In interviews with high school students, participants evaluated particular school policies and practices in relation to students' ideas about what "regular" schools were supposed to be like and do. As a result, they presented complex and occasionally conflicting explanations of whether school policies and practices were "fair" that did not necessarily align with whether those policies and practices directly seemed to support or harm the participants themselves. In these ways, participants considered whether their schools were legitimate or not more often than they described direct ways in which their schools supported or harmed them and their classmates.

Across interviews, participants explained that the main, most legitimate purpose of school was to support students academically. Participants spoke favorably of policies and practices that seemed most directly related to that purpose, whether those policies and practices actually seemed to support students' academic achievement or not. When participants described policies and practices that seemed to them to be less directly linked to academics (e.g., dress codes or cell phone policies), they expressed more ambivalence about those practices or rejected them outright. As an adult and a teacher, I can see how some of the school rules participants described were meant to deter students from engaging in behavior that would impact their learning—behaviors like coming to school high or coming to school late. However, these rules lost legitimacy to students when the punishments themselves interfered with students' abilities to learn by removing students from class.

For example, one participant argued that school rules and disciplinary practices should only be related to doing academic work. This student explained that the rules at their school included, "No chewing gum. Even though most of us still do that. No hoodies in the classroom. Can't wear sweaters . . . can't have your cellphone, not allowed to. Can't, um, be on your phone while you're in class" and no "headphones in our ears." When asked what they thought of those rules, this participant explained, "most of that is stupid—I say. Because, really, if I'm doing my work?" then the rules don't make sense. This student introduces the idea of whether or not students are doing academic work as the central question that schools should be asking, and then argues that students who are doing work should not be saddled with peripheral rules. This participant also explained that rules should protect other students' ability to do academic work, noting that if kids listened to music on headphones while working, they would "make sure it's not too loud."

Another participant explained that the school's "business" was only to help students complete academic work and that, as a result, there should only be consequences for unfinished work or missing classes. For example, this participant said that it was unfair of the school to suspend them when they came to school under the influence of drugs, "Cause, I'm still coming to school. At the end of the day . . . it's just not the school's business. It just should—leave me be." This participant explained that "coming to school" was the most important criterion schools should be using in deciding whether to address student behavior, and that the school overreached in suspending them frequently, particularly because this student "noticed that I missed a lot of schoolwork within the—these past three years that past. I wish I was going to school." Although the school probably linked students coming to school high with students' academic performance, this connection was not clear to the student, particularly when the school's response so clearly interfered with this participant's ability to learn by removing the student from school. At one charter school this participant had attended, the majority of students had been suspended at least once during the year the student was in attendance. This student argued that it would be better for the school to use academic consequences for behavioral infractions instead, suggesting that, if a student was disruptive or not completing work: "You gotta make up that class."

Other participants also argued that consequences of breaking rules were unfair when those consequences interfered with academic work. For example, one student explained that the school was too strict in its enforcement of the lateness policy, in ways that interfered with students' ability to do well in their classes. They explained that students are expected to arrive at school by 8:20 or face consequences for being late: "You come in latest is 8:20? That means you still early, but anything after 8:20? I mean, 8:21, like, I came in like 8:21. Anything after that? You're considered late." The student here expresses their disbelief at how strictly the school differentiates between 8:20, which is "still early" and 8:21, which is already "late." This school required students who were late to wait in the in-school suspension room until the next period rather than disrupting class by entering late. This practice caused this student to miss first period whenever they came to school later than 8:20, which meant that students missed the entire class regardless of whether they arrived at 8:21 or 9:00.

Participants' insistence that punishments that interfered with learning are "stupid" helps shed light on the large body of literature that suggests that zero-tolerance policies can be counterproductive, making behavior worse among both students who are punished and their peers (e.g., Burt, 2014; Hines-Datiri & Andrews, 2017; Skiba et al., 2014) since removing students from learning opportunities challenges the legitimacy of the school as an institution whose purpose is to promote academic achievement. This finding also helps explain research that suggests exclusionary disciplinary policies create negative school climates by diminishing the perceived legitimacy of schools and school staff among students. This diminished legitimacy seemed to make the rules themselves illegitimate to students as well. Although school staff probably had good reasons for not wanting kids to listen to music during some work periods, come to school high, or come to school late, participants saw the punishments (e.g., missing all of first period) as more harmful to their learning than the behaviors themselves (e.g., coming to first period ten minutes late), which made them suspicious of the rules as well.

NYC SCHOOLS AND THE STPP

Students receiving special education services will have very different experiences in different schools related to school types (e.g., D75 or charter), policies, practices, structures, and curricula. Of course, kids within the same school may have very different experiences as well, but it is outside the scope of this book to address that in detail. In other words, this section explores directly risky and indirectly risky school policies and practices within and across the NYC public school system. In this section, I will describe some school-level factors that predict an increased likelihood of students with IEPs being arrested. These analyses use administrative data from all 1,074 public middle and high schools in NYC during the 2013–2014 school year. The data set and methods of analysis are described further in Appendix B.

I began by running descriptive statistics for the sample as a whole, then separately for schools that did or did not have at least one student with an IEP who had been arrested ("YesArrest" or "NoArrest" schools). These descriptive statistics begin to suggest some differences between YesArrest and NoArrest Schools. For example, the average number of days students are absent in YesArrest schools was 25 days per year, while at NoArrest schools students were absent an average of almost sixteen days per year. The average percent of students with disabilities in YesArrest schools is 27.5 percent, while at NoArrest schools it is 20.7 percent (table 3.2).

Next, I used regression analysis to determine which school-level factors statistically significantly predicted an increased likelihood of being a YesArrest school using various models, and considered how existing research might explain these relationships. The remainder of this chapter addresses the school-level factors that appeared statistically significant in my analyses (table 3.3).

Table 3.2   Descriptive Statistics for NYC Public Middle and High Schools

	All Schools	YesArrest Schools	NoArrest Schools
Average student days absent	19.0141	25.1	15.6
Percent that are charters	9.0	2.9	12.3
Percent that are D75 schools	5.0	8.1	3.3
Percent that are D79 schools	0.0	0.0	0.0
Percent that are community schools	86.0	89.1	84.3
ELL percent	12.9544	13.0	12.9
Poverty percent	77.6378	79.8	76.4
White percent	9.0646	6.2	10.7
Black percent	38.4163	41.4	36.8
Latinx percent	42.2795	44.2	41.2
Asian percent	9.1091	7.1	10.2
Native American percent	.6053	.7	.6
Percent of students in CTT classes	7.0696	8.7	6.1
Percent of students in alternative classes	.0915	.0	.1
Percent of students in self-contained classes	8.9354	12.2	7.1
Students with disabilities: percent of total	23.1178	27.5	20.7
Percent students suspended 1or more times	3.026	3.1	3.0
Number of years teaching	40.544	8.1	8.0
Percent teachers no valid certification	2.352	1.3	3.0
Percent teachers out of certification	18.917	21.1	17.7
Percent teachers <3 years experience	18.192	17.1	18.8
Percent teachers masters + 30 credits	38.599	41.1	37.2
Percent teachers not "highly qualified"	13.751	15.2	13.0
Percent staff turnover: within 5 years	21.038	22.9	20.0
Percent staff turnover: ever	20.723	21.3	20.0
Percent passed ELA test	38.9280	39.5	38.6
Percent passed math test	36.1097	32.0	38.3
Survey results: academic expectations	8.0759	7.9	8.2
Survey results: communication	7.9303	7.8	8.0
Survey results: student engagement	7.5811	7.4	7.7
Survey results: safety	7.7033	7.4	7.9
School age (years)	13.0778	15.6	14.78

Table 3.3   Odds Ratios YesArrest: NoArrest Schools

	Model 1	Model 2	Model 3	Model 4
Average student days absent	1.050	1.060	1.111	1.061
Charter school	X			
D75 school	X			
ELL percent	X			
Poverty percent	X			
White percent	X			
Black percent	X			
Latinx percent	X			
Asian percent	X			
Native American percent	X			
Multirace percent	X			
Percent of students in CTT classes	1.063	1.053	1.045	1.062
Percent of students in alternative classes	X			
Students with disabilities: percent of total	X			
Percent students suspended 1 or more times	1.042	1.101	X	1.134
Percent teachers no valid certification	X			
Percent teachers out of certification	X			
Percent teachers <3 years experience	X			
Percent teachers masters + 30 credits	1.026	1.009	X	X
Percent teachers not "highly qualified"	X			
Teacher years in DOE		1.048		
Teacher mean days absent		1.066		
Percent passed ELA test		1.018		
Percent passed math test		0.983		
Survey results: academic expectations			X	
Survey results: communication			-1.235	
Survey results: student engagement			1.827	
Survey results: safety			-1.217	
School age				1

Note: an "X" means that variable did not significantly predict an increased likelihood that a school was a YesArrest school $P < 0.05$ in that model.

Average Number of Student Days Absent

Research suggests that student absences negatively affect academic achievement, and that these negative effects are not entirely related to lost instructional time, but may also result from disruptions to teaching and learning that occur when students miss lessons and are caught up (or not) by their teachers (Goodman, 2014). This study builds upon that research by suggesting that schools with high levels of student absences may also be more likely to have had students with IEPs who have been arrested, although more research is necessary to better understand how and why.

Percent of Students (with and without IEPs) in Collaborative Team Teaching Classes

Collaborative team teaching (CTT) classes have become increasingly popular in many districts, including NYC, for improving the educational experiences and outcomes of students with and without disabilities. However, research suggests that there are diverse manifestations of "co-teaching" practices within officially labeled co-teaching classrooms (Rivera et al., 2014). This variation may result from varying types and levels of administrative support, as well as differences in teachers' attitudes toward collaborative teaching (Damore & Murray, 2009) across and within certification areas (e.g., general or special education). This study suggests that CTT classes are not a panacea for students with or without IEPs, but more research is necessary to better understand what, exactly, is occurring in classes that are coded as CTT classes. For example, teachers I know who teach CTT classes in NYC often describe them as being large (thirty to thirty-five students), which would make it very difficult to deliver the individualized support that any adolescent with (or without) an IEP needs.

In addition, these data do not show whether students in the CTT classes are the ones getting arrested; it is possible that schools that rely heavily on CTT classes are different in other important ways from other schools. It is possible that schools which educate most students in the CTT model also maintain separate classes for students considered to have the most "severe" disabilities, and that those students receive a substantially different education from their peers in the CTT classes.

Percent of Students Who Were Suspended at Least Once

Research suggests that high suspension rates may negatively affect the experiences of both students who are directly affected and of other students who have not been suspended. Students who have been suspended lose instructional time (Gregory et al., 2010), while the negative school climate that results from heavy reliance on exclusionary punishments such as suspensions negatively affects both students who have and have not been suspended (Rocque & Paternoster, 2011; Smalls et al., 2007). This study suggests another link between suspensions and arrest.

Percent of Teachers with Highest Education Level

The connection between an increased percentage of teachers with their master's degree plus 30 additional credits and a higher likelihood of a school being a YesArrest school is more difficult to explain. Because all variables are school-level variables, it is possible that the most highly educated teachers in these schools do not teach students receiving special education services, and that schools with higher percentages of highly educated teachers also have wider discrepancies between young people with and without IEPs in both experiences and outcomes.

Test Scores

The percent of students who passed an ELA standardized test (out of all students who took an ELA test) during the 2013–2014 school-year significantly predicted an increased likelihood of a school being a YesArrest school. The percent of students who passed a Math standardized test that year statistically significantly predicted a lower likelihood of a school being a YesArrest school.

Finding an inverse relationship between ELA pass rates and the likelihood of being a YesArrest school builds upon research that suggests that test scores have limited ability to describe the overall quality of a school. NYC, like most districts across the country, uses tests that are high-stakes for both students and schools. Students who do not pass Regents examinations in high school cannot get a high school diploma, regardless of how well they did in their classes. In addition, NYC schools with low pass rates experience increased surveillance, reduced ability to make curriculum decisions, and threat of closure (Riehl et al., 2018), all of which can be demoralizing for teachers and students (Hoogland et al., 2016). Using tests for accountability purposes has led to schools, districts, and states "gaming the system" by, for example, narrowing curricula to focus on tested subjects or excluding low-performing students from taking tests by suspending them, expelling them, or simply encouraging them to stay home (Amrein-Beardsley, 2009; Kim et al., 2010). More research is necessary to determine what, specifically, is happening at schools with higher English pass rates that predict an increased likelihood of those schools being YesArrest schools. Regardless, these results suggest that state test scores alone cannot tell us everything we may want to know about a school's ability to support its students.

Further, schools are legally able to exclude many students from taking state tests, including up to one to two percent of each district that is considered to have disabilities too "severe" to make standardized testing a good option for assessing student learning. Students who are newly learning English may also be exempt from standardized tests like the Regents. Categorically excluding groups of students who have traditionally been marginalized within schools (students who are considered to have the most severe disabilities and novice ELLs) makes it difficult to assess how well schools are educating *all* students. However, critiques about the ableist and culturally biased nature of large-scale assessments (e.g., Au, 2013; Harris-Murri et al., 2006) reflect even greater difficulties in connecting these test scores directly to high-quality, culturally relevant instruction.

School Climate Survey Results

Higher average school climate survey score on questions related to student engagement predicted an increased likelihood of YesArrest schools, while higher average school climate survey scores on questions related to communicating with families and how safe schools seem each predicted a decreased likelihood of a school being a YesArrest school.

The finding of an inverse relationship between student engagement scores and YesArrest status is surprising given research suggesting that student engagement is an important predictor of many positive outcomes such as academic achievement (Khalifa, 2011), reduced truancy (Fallis & Opotow, 2003), and staying in school until graduation (Christle et al., 2007). One possible reason for this surprising finding is that students receiving special education services may have substantively different experiences at these schools; in fact, those students may be reporting lower levels of engagement than their peers. The school-level variables used in this study aggregate scores across all students; more research is necessary to further explore how students with and without IEPs may perceive the same school differently.

These findings build upon existing research suggesting that engaging and communicating with families correlates with positive outcomes for students with disabilities (Haber et al., 2016). In addition, these findings build upon existing research suggesting that students' perceptions of school safety correlates with students' feeling that they are connected to their schools and able to learn (Zullig et al., 2017). Specifically, this study suggests that negative perceptions of family involvement and school safety are significant predictors of YesArrest schools.

DISCUSSION

Efforts to reform NYC public schools and provide responsive, specialized schools to meet the needs of a diverse student body have been constrained by the same pressures that schools all over the U.S. face. The need to appear legitimate is particularly important for special education, which suffers from low status within a low status field. When high school students who had received special education services and been arrested talked about what helped or hindered them at school, they drew upon discourses around what "regular" schools are supposed to be like to assess the legitimacy of a particular practice rather than describing how that practice affected them more directly. This finding builds upon research suggesting that schools' needs to maintain legitimacy among stakeholders (including students) may cause them to enact policies and practices that aren't in the best interests of their students. This chapter also identified some school-level factors that statistically significantly predict increased (or decreased) likelihood of students with IEPs in NYC public middle and high schools getting arrested during one school year. The following chapter will explore in more detail how some high school students who have received special education services and been arrested think about and evaluate adults and peers at their schools.

Chapter 4

Young People Talk about and around Special Educators and Peers with IEPs

"I try not to be distracted by other people."—Participant reflecting on making friends at a D75 high school

Disability rights activists have long argued, "nothing about us without us"—any research, policy, programs, etc. that is about people with disabilities must incorporate the perspectives of people with disabilities. However, research on the education of students with disabilities rarely asks kids receiving special education services to talk about their experiences. Education research, in general, rarely asks kids how they make sense of what's happening in their classrooms and schools. Before beginning the study that forms the basis of much of this book, I assumed that this lack of research was purely a reflection of biases about the value of kids' perspectives. However, as I describe in more detail in Appendix A, many rules and regulations that are intended to protect "vulnerable populations" (e.g., kids, people with disabilities, and/or incarcerated people) make it extremely time-consuming and difficult to talk with kids who have received special education services and been arrested. For many researchers who are under time pressures (e.g., to complete a dissertation or earn tenure), the delays associated with this type of research can be a huge deterrent. Social science research involving adults has recently moved to reduce restrictions around certain types of research that present very low risks to participants (e.g., asking teachers to talk about their practice); it would be tremendously helpful if federal guidelines also identified some minimal-risk activities for kids (e.g., talking about their schools) and facilitated that kind of research while still ensuring that safeguards to preserve confidentiality remained in place.

If I had known how long it would take to complete the interview portion of this study, I might have put it off for a safer time in my career—and may never have actually conducted these interviews. I am certainly glad that I did, though, since they surprised me in many ways. Before beginning interviews, I assumed that the data I collected would be fairly straightforward—kids who had received special education services in New York City public schools and subsequently been arrested would give me a list of things that they did or did not find helpful about their schools, and explain why. However, these interviews caused me to rethink the way that we evaluate schools, school policies, and school practices, as I began describing in the previous chapter and will describe further in this chapter.

As a teacher, I was often struck by how differently my students interpreted classroom events from how I did and, as a result, how my attempts to help my students might be perceived as harmful instead. For example, I once asked a high school student to come talk with me outside the classroom. My rationale, which I did not initially articulate to her, was that I needed to have a slightly longer conversation with her about a personal matter, so I did not want to disturb her classmates, who were working silently, or to allow anyone else to overhear her private business. She refused to come outside with me. After some discussion, I discovered that she associated being asked to step outside with being in trouble. Even after I explained that she was not, in fact, in trouble—that I just wanted to talk to her privately without disturbing her classmates—she still wanted to remain in the classroom to talk since she was worried that a dean or other member of the school staff would see her talking to me in the hall and assume the worst. My assumption that talking in the hall would help this student by preserving her privacy was challenged by the student's assumption that talking in the hall would harm her by giving the administration the impression that she had done something wrong. There are many opportunities for misunderstandings like this to arise throughout the school day, and, unfortunately, not always enough time to get to the bottom of each one.

The interviews I conducted with high school students (ages fifteen to twenty-one, in ninth to twelfth grade) also frequently caused me to rethink my assumptions about how kids make sense of what is—and is not—for their benefit at school. For example, I expected most participants to be critical of certain school practices, like suspension, that are widely seen as harmful in the existing research. However, the ubiquity of many of those practices—like suspension—gave them legitimacy and, as a result, made them seem like a "fair" response even when participants described ways in which they had personally been harmed by those practices. Participants tended to blame themselves for unhelpful school practices rather than questioning the legitimacy of common practices.

This chapter builds upon discussions of legitimacy and risk to make sense of the complex and occasionally contradictory ways in which the kids I spoke with described adults and peers they interacted with at school. Building upon my argument that special education services are perceived as less legitimate, and students with individualized education programs (IEPs) are perceived as posing a risk to schools and classmates, I argue in this chapter that kids receiving special education services and their teachers must navigate the *stigma* associated with disability as they navigate relationships with adults and other kids at school. This stigma does not only affect kids who are receiving special education services themselves, but also the adults who work with them—teachers, paraprofessionals, deans, related service providers (e.g., speech therapists), and administrators.

NAVIGATING STIGMA AND STIGMATIZED IDENTITIES

Although many argue that special education is a benevolent institution, intended to give extra, "special" support to some kids at school, many people, including special education teachers and students with IEPs, don't necessarily see special education services as a desirable institution to be part of. Special education has historically had, and continues to have, a hard time recruiting and retaining teachers, particularly in middle and high schools. Further, kids receiving special education services often feel ashamed of those services rather than grateful for them (see, e.g., an excellent spoken word poem on this subject by high school student Amir Bilal Billups). The fact that the people who are supposed to benefit from a particular arrangement don't necessarily see that arrangement as helpful is a problem that needs to be addressed. As I will argue in more detail in chapter 6, I don't think it's possible to maintain separate but equal systems for kids with and without disabilities, and think that inclusive, accessible education for all is the best response to the stigma associated with special education (as well as other persistent problems with special education). However, for those who are committed to maintain a dual system of special and general education, or for all of us who are working within this system until it is dismantled, understanding the ways in which young people navigate the stigma associated with special education will help adults better understand why our students may react in surprising ways to the things that we or their peers do.

Link and Phelan (2001) argue that stigma results from four interrelated factors: (1) distinguishing and labeling difference; (2) associating difference with negative attributes; (3) separating "us" from "them" according to this difference; and (4) status loss of and discrimination against people with this particular difference. These processes all describe exactly what happens when a child is identified as having an "educational disability:" the child is given a label that is considered less desirable (e.g., "emotionally disturbed" rather than "gifted" or even "typically developing"), and frequently separated for at least part of the school day into a separate part of the classroom or separate setting entirely where they engage in lower-status activities (e.g., read a shorter book than their classmates).

Link and Phelan (2001) further argue that many efforts to reduce stigma focus on changing a particular behavior, but don't necessarily change people's beliefs or the power differentials between groups. For example, while I was teaching, the official classification of some of my students changed from "mental retardation" to "intellectual disability" in an effort to reduce the stigma associated with "the r word." This is not the first time that labels within special education have changed. It sounds appalling now to think about calling children "mentally defective" or "feebleminded," but, in the absence of larger changes in attitudes and practices, it seems likely to me that the term "intellectual disability" will eventually take on the same baggage and negative associations as previous terms since many people still hold negative biases and stereotypes about people with intellectual disabilities. On the other hand, some movements have tried to reclaim stigmatized terms like "queer" or "crip" in order to try to change people's attitudes about those groups more directly by pointing out that there is nothing actually wrong with what these terms signify. It might be more fruitful to push back on negative stereotypes about people with intellectual disabilities and to change practices that keep people with these types of disabilities separate from others without those types of disabilities than to keep changing the label used.

Disability Studies (DS), among other theories, points out that people often reduce the full range of human complexity and diversity into binaries, e.g., male and female; White people and people of color; or native and immigrant. Many people do not fit neatly into these categories (e.g., people who are intersex, trans, or biracial), and there is great diversity within each category (e.g., both American-born people and immigrants speak a range of languages, practice a range of religions, and belong to a range of socioeconomic statuses). However, these binaries serve to create hierarchies, with a more and less stigmatized category contrasted against each other. For example, people who are categorized as "male" or "White" experience less discrimination than people who are categorized as "female," "nonbinary," or "people of color."

Similarly, our education system sorts and labels kids using the binary general education and special education. This reflects an assumption that some kids are "normal" or "typically developing," while others are "abnormal" or "atypical." These assumptions disregard the wide range of abilities and inabilities that are present across any group of humans. Further, this binary is also perceived as hierarchical: general education is a higher status form of education than special education, which means that those who are associated with special education must navigate stigma. Efforts to integrate kids with and without disabilities in the same classrooms tend to suggest that general education is the best place for all students to be, that students without IEPs are the most desirable type of classmates, and that this integration primarily benefits kids with IEPs. Different disability labels have different levels of stigma associated with them, with high-incidence labels like "emotional disturbance," or mild "intellectual disability" being among the most stigmatized. As a result, many students have to navigate multiple levels of stigma related to disability and disability classifications.

Just as the kids I spoke with compared their schools to an imagined "regular" school to evaluate the legitimacy of their school's policies and practices, the students I spoke with evaluated school staff and peers with IEPs in relation to their assumptions about what teachers at "regular" schools do and how "normal" high school students behave. In other words, the high school students I interviewed did not simply describe and evaluate school staff's and peers' actions in relation to how much they helped or harmed participants. For example, the participant who tried "not to get distracted by other people" in order to focus on their schoolwork in the quote that opens this chapter also described a lonely, friendless existence at their D75 (special education) high school. This student frequently cut school, missing weeks or even months of instruction and assignments. Although there are probably many reasons that this student avoided school, the lack of relationships with classmates couldn't have helped this student feel motivated to come in.

"BE THE BEST TEACHER YOU CAN BE!": THE ROLE OF ADULTS AT SCHOOL

Just as participants' schools were evaluated in relation to imagined "regular" schools, school staff were evaluated as much based on their conformity to young people's ideas about what school staff's legitimate roles or "business" are as on how school staff's actions actually impacted kids. All of the young people I spoke with argued that school staff's primary and most legitimate role should involve supporting students' academic growth (school staff mentioned by participants included teachers, paraprofessionals, deans, and counselors, but many of the findings could also apply to other related services providers and administrators). When school staff tried to support students in nonacademic matters, three students described at least some of those examples as overreaching. Participants seemed to make sense of academic support as within the scope of "regular" schools' roles and functions, and, as a result, as positive.

On the other hand, when school staff tried to address kids' behavior, feelings, or interpersonal relationships, students were much more critical of these staff actions, particularly when school staff tried to address behaviors that participants did not perceive to be clearly linked to learning (e.g., wearing a hoodie). Although many teachers, researchers, and policy makers agree that it's necessary and valuable to support kids' nonacademic needs, the students receiving special education services who I spoke with were suspicious of these goals, worrying that nonacademic support was part of the "special" education they were receiving.

During my first year as a teacher, I was hired to do "push in" and "pull out" at a private school that was newly implementing more inclusion of kids with IEPs in the general education classroom. My role was to make any relevant accommodations to the existing curriculum in English, Social Studies, and Science for my students (all of the seventh and eighth graders with IEPs), support my students in the general education classroom, and teach self-contained "study skills" classes for my students to give them extra support in these areas. Although every young first-year teacher faces challenges, my students and colleagues frequently expressed the belief that my role was mainly to make things easier for my students (e.g., to select 10 words from the list of 20 vocabulary words for my students to be responsible for) and that, as a result, any changes I made to materials or activities were necessarily making things worse. As excited as I was to enact what I had learned in my newly completed masters program in Language and Literacy Education, my students clamored to fill out the same vocabulary definition worksheets as their classmates rather than studying vocabulary in the context of complex texts since any work assigned by the general education teachers was perceived to be more legitimate than any work I assigned. My colleagues who teach "advanced" students engage in many of the same practices I was trying to implement, but those actions are interpreted differently by students and colleagues within the context of an "honors" class than in a special education class.

Research suggests that special educators must navigate their particular positions within the hierarchies of education and educators, as well as their own and others' perceptions of them as people with "specialized expertise" but also as people who face stigma based on their work with a stigmatized population (Roegman et al., 2017). It is outside the scope of this book to address the complex ways that adults with and without disabilities navigate the stigma associated with working with youth with IEPs, but the interviews I conducted suggest that young people were aware of the stigma facing special educators and, as a result, were critical of any actions that seemed too far outside the scope of what they imagined "regular" teachers to do. Although teachers in general education do also mentor and advise the young people they work with on a range of topics beyond the specific academic goals of the day, students receiving special education services associated nonacademic guidance with "special" behavioral support.

Although participants expressed skepticism about many actions by school staff that were not clearly and directly connected to academics, five of the seven participants also explained that, under particular circumstances, adults at school could and did earn the right to expand their default roles to include nonacademic support, including advising students about their behavior. In this way, participants seemed to distinguish between "the school," with its inherently limited role (i.e., academic support) on the one hand, and particular adults who needed to be providers of academic support but could also occupy additional roles. Specifically, as I describe further in this section, school staff had to: (1) establish their legitimacy through their willingness and ability to provide academic support; and then (2) develop personal relationships with students in order to advise and guide students on nonacademic matters. Although many researchers and educators emphasize the importance of caring relationships between adults and students at school (e.g., Gay, 2010), it is worth emphasizing that participants in this study described academic support as the most important and legitimate element of school staff's care.

School Staff Should Focus Primarily on Academic Support

When presenting and explaining how adults helped them at school, participants all foregrounded academic assistance and expressed appreciation for staff who supported students' academic growth. For example, one participant said that the best thing about their school was "the teachers. They support us." This student further described teachers' support as, "they make sure you understand it," emphasizing academic support. In describing advice to a hypothetical new student, this participant said the student should, "just work your hardest . . . because they've got high expectations. That's it." This student, like other participants, described expecting teachers to lay out academic expectations and make sure students understand the academic work.

Three participants also credited teachers with promoting their academic growth by making subjects they normally did not like more interesting. For these participants, their teachers' roles were not just to explain academic concepts but also to make academic work engaging and relevant to promote student success. These students' perspectives reflect research suggesting that student engagement is a strong influence on academic performance (Smalls et al., 2007). For example, one participant said that their favorite class was math, then clarified: "I liked it when [a particular teacher] was here. [She] made it, like, fun. Like, I hate math. But she made it fun for me." Although this student claimed to "hate math," this student credited a favorite teacher with making math "fun" so that this student was motivated to work hard and pass the Algebra I Regents.

Most participants described appreciating teachers who took the initiative to offer academic support to students who might be reticent about asking for it. For example, one participant explained that a favorite science teacher gave them "extra help" and explained, "At first, she was coming to me, and then that's when I—I started taking the help and then I started asking her." Once this student saw that the teacher was willing and able to help them academically, this student began making an effort to "get there [to school] a little bit earlier, just in case I got a test." When asked for a particular example of a time this teacher helped this student out, the participant said that they had been running behind on a science fair project, "and one morning, she [the teacher]— she had half of the project ready for me. Like, she did half of it already. I just needed to do the other half." This teacher created conditions that encouraged the student to complete some of the work on the project instead of simply giving the student a failing grade and having the student complete no work.

However, one participant argued that teachers could offer too much academic support, explaining, "I don't like asking for help. I like knowing stuff on my own . . . It's like playing a game. You try to figure it out, they try to give you a hint, but you don't want to take it. You want to figure it out for yourself . . . Take the easy way? I like to take the hard way." This student takes prides in taking "the hard way" and also compares the satisfaction of solving a math problem without help to winning a game without needing hints. Providing students with the right level of academic support is complex, so teachers can provide options for when and how students can access varying types and levels of academic support.

In addition to valuing academic support, participants spoke negatively about school staff who seemed to prioritize managing students' behavior at the expense of academic support. Although researchers and teachers generally see student learning as the end goal of behavior management (Wolff et al., 2017), participants in this study described not always seeing a clear link between staff addressing student behavior and academic achievement. When participants did not see a clear link to academic support, participants described behavioral support as overreaching and found it to be illegitimate.

For example, one student spoke negatively about teachers who spent a lot of time in class handling behavioral problems, since that time detracted from academic instruction. When asked what advice they would give a new teacher at their school, that participant said, "don't listen to what the kids say! I mean, you're the teacher . . . just focus, you know? Be a teacher! Be the best teacher you can be." This participant's advice to "Be a teacher!" suggests a definitive and clear role for the teacher, even though this participant does not fully define that role. However, one important aspect of "being a teacher" involves staying on task and focusing on academics rather than getting bogged down in classroom management.

Without exception, participants spoke positively of teachers offering academic support, and explained that academic support was the most important part of teachers' roles, although students varied somewhat in how they conceptualized the right academic supports. This finding builds upon many approaches to education that suggest that promoting students' learning and academic growth is always the most important purpose of teachers; that purpose should not be lost or obscured in the context of pursuing other worthwhile goals such as teaching for social justice (e.g., Cochran-Smith et al., 2009) or developing students' cultural competence (e.g., Ladson-Billings, 2014).

Nonacademic Support: When It Is and Is Not Well Received

Once school staff had demonstrated their willingness to support students' academic achievement, the high school students I spoke with were more willing to accept nonacademic guidance from those adults as well. Four of the seven participants explained that they accepted nonacademic guidance from adults who also supported them academically, particularly when those adults also formed personal relationships with students. These adults might engage in "positive harassment" (Duncan-Andrade, 2009), or persistent insistence that students be their best selves, including academic achievement but also behavioral and moral standards. Otherwise, three of the seven participants described rejecting nonacademic guidance from adults who did not already support students academically and develop personal relationships with students. Duncan-Andrade's use of the term "positive harassment" acknowledges the overlap in many behaviors between actions that students view in a "positive" light versus those that may seem more like "harassment." To participants in this study, the most important distinction between adults' behaviors being seen positively versus negatively included the existence of a trusting relationship between the adult and students and clear connections between adult guidance and benefits to the student (as opposed to, e.g., adults trying to assert their own authority).

One student explained that school staff who supported students academically had credibility when advising students about behavior. This participant described favorite teachers as those who "don't take crap from the students, but also they'll help you complete stuff." Because these favorite adults helped the student with academic work, this participant accepted their strict behavioral expectations as clearly related to getting schoolwork done and, as a result, as legitimate.

Another student also said that they appreciated nonacademic guidance from teachers who also supported them academically. One teacher was their favorite because "he just helps with math and stuff. Like, and if you have any problems." The academic guidance was presented first, but then the student also expressed appreciating this teacher's help with "any" problems. When asked what advice they would give a new teacher at their school, this student also suggested that teachers should also go beyond supporting students academically. This participant said that they would tell a new teacher, "try to be out there, just to be out there with your students . . . go farther each day" with "everything," not just with academic work. Although this participant foregrounds the academic support they received, they also appreciate teachers who help with "everything" else as well.

One participant explained how they interpreted virtually identical non-academic guidance very differently when it came from different teachers who were or were not able to successfully link their guidance to academic achievement. In describing favorite teachers, this student explained that, "say, like you trying to be a thug . . . they gonna let you know, listen, you ain't no thug. You ain't none of this, cause you really about that. You gonna do this, or whatnot. I say yeah." Here, this participant describes appreciating and following advice ("I say yeah") from teachers who convey the positive expectation that this student is "really about" doing well at school. However, this participant later describes their least favorite teachers similarly, saying "I don't like when teachers act tough and then trying—trying to say yo, you not a thug, that. Listen, you don't know what I been through. You don't know about my life, my past." This assertion that the student is not really a "thug" takes on various meanings from different teachers depending on how well the teachers establish their guidance as being intended to support the student's academic growth versus "act[ing] tough" or trying to establish teachers' own authority. Further, the different nature of the relationships between the two teachers and this student causes the first teacher to seem like the teacher knows what this student is "really about," whereas the second teacher doesn't "know about [the student's] life."

Another participant rejected a teacher's attempts to manage the student's behavior by reaching out to the student's family and other school staff. Although school–home partnerships can be helpful to students, it seems like this teacher may have skipped the step of establishing and developing a relationship with this participant. This participant described their least favorite teacher as a "snitch," explaining, "If I'm disrupting her class . . . she texts my family member at that moment. Or she gonna tell the principal." This student explained that "I stopped going to her class. And I stopped doing work in her class" because that teacher "snitched for everything," further emphasizing that the "snitching" "was just the main reason" they stopped attending class. This student acknowledged "disrupting her class," so the disagreement was not about what happened. Instead, the student explained that they disliked how the teacher responded without speaking directly to the student. Rather than altering their behavior in this class, the participant started avoiding it altogether to prevent these tense encounters.

Participants' descriptions of when and why they accepted school staff's nonacademic guidance builds upon research suggesting that engaging instruction and strong academic support by itself can reduce the amount of time school staff spends on addressing student behavior (e.g., McIntosh et al., 2018). In addition, research suggests strong, trusting relationships between students and staff are necessary for providing behavioral support to adolescent students (e.g., Gregory & Ripski, 2008). These trusting relationships form the basis of school staff's authority when providing nonacademic guidance, which participants considered to be otherwise outside the scope of school staff's roles and responsibilities. The clear connections to academic achievement and strong, trusted relationships may be particularly important for students receiving special education services who may otherwise view nonacademic supports as illegitimate and outside the scope of "regular schools" roles.

AMBIVALENCE ABOUT PEERS

Several of the high school students I spoke with described seeing friends as a highlight of their time at particular schools. For example, when I asked one participant what it was like being a student at a school they had attended, they replied, "I love my friends. My friends go [to that school], so . . . If I do go to new school, different school, I'ma kinda be sad, you know." However, participants' descriptions of their peers were not all positive. Five of the seven high school students I spoke with described at least some of their peers as potentially harmful distractions from academic success. Specifically, four of the seven participants argued that other students with IEPs might hinder their success at school. However, each participant also described ways in which peers helped them at school, suggesting ways in which peer relationships can actually support students as well. When participants only, or primarily, interacted with other students with IEPs in D75 schools or self-contained special education classes, participants described navigating between the perceived negatives of associating with peers with IEPs and the real downsides of not having friends at school. This perceived dilemma reflects the stigma associated with disability and the negative assumption that kids with IEPs pose risks to other students and are not valuable friends for other kids.

In presenting and explaining how peers helped or hindered them, participants introduced the idea that there are categories, or types, of students, then positioned themselves and other students within those categories. Research suggests that the ways in which school staff and others respond to different students exhibiting the same behaviors, or to different student behaviors, leads students (and adults) to sort and hierarchically categorize their peers (e.g., Collins, 2011; Youdell, 2006). This sense of hierarchy is magnified by formal categorizing and sorting processes, like assigning a disability classification or putting a child in a separate classroom from peers for part or all of the day.

Participants in this study explicitly referred to two categories of students: students with disabilities and troublemakers ("the type of kids to just start trouble"). Students with disabilities and students who "start trouble" sometimes overlapped in participants' descriptions, suggesting that the students I spoke with had internalized some of the stereotypes about students receiving special education services as posing risks to peers. These categories were implicitly defined in relation to "normal" students. One feature of the category "normal students" is that it is defined primarily in opposition to other categories, but not usually explicitly named or interrogated (e.g., Ferri, 2009). Participants suggested that these categories were hierarchical; kids with IEPs or troublemakers were not as desirable as friends as "normal" students.

The assumptions that students with disabilities and/or "troublemakers" are not desirable friends is layered on top of the common assumption that middle and high school students, in general, are more likely to have negative influences on each other than positive ones (Tierney & Colyar, 2005). However, participants also described ways in which their peers supported them academically, reflecting research that shows the many ways in which adolescents provide important sources of support for each other at school (e.g., Knight & Marciano, 2013), even when schools do not explicitly encourage such support (e.g., Villalpondo & Solarzano, 2005). The next section will explore the complex ways in which participants described their peers as perceived and real distractions and resources. The following two sections will look specifically at how participants talked about: (1) students with IEPs versus other students and (2) troublemakers versus students who get into trouble.

Peer Relationships as Distractions and Resources

The majority of participants described at least some of their peers as potentially harmful distractions at school. For example, one participant who attended a D75 school explained that, "I focus on myself. So I can get outta here and graduate. I don't pay attention to nobody else." This participant further described never studying or socializing with peers at school. However, most participants complicated the idea that peers could not contribute anything valuable. For example, another participant said they similarly would advise other students to, "Just stick to yourself. Focus on school" in order to be successful. Nevertheless, this participant also described enjoying time at a zoned community school because their friends had attended that school, saying that the community school, "was cool. It was like, you know, people I knew from my neighborhood. So it was—I was—it was cool. I liked being there." This participant presents peers as a potential distraction, but also as resource that made school more enjoyable.

Some participants went further and attributed going to school (or not) to having friends (or not). To these participants, peers were linked to academic success by serving as an incentive to attend school. For example, one participant explained that that they had initially avoided going to a D75 school they had transferred to, "cause I didn't like coming. I didn't like—when I came here, I didn't know nobody. So I didn't want to be here. It was like, ugh, I don't want to come. So I just started cutting." This participant later made friends and enjoyed school, and explicitly connected having positive peer relationships to increased attendance. This participant made this association despite also arguing that students were placed in that D75 school because of their (bad) "attitudes."

Adults at participants' schools contributed to participants' senses both that their peers might pose risks to them, and that they might pose risks to their peers. For example, one participant who attended a co-located D75 school (which shared a building with other, non-D75 schools) explained that a rule was, "Can't talk to people from the other . . . like, other different schools. I'm saying, what? It makes no sense . . . That's how you know this is, difference between this school and a regular school." This participant described a perception that students from the D75 school, in particular, were supposed to stay separate from peers at other schools in the building.

STUDENTS WITH IEPS VERSUS OTHER STUDENTS

Although all participants in this study had received some sort of special education services, the four participants who spoke most explicitly about their experiences with special education frequently differentiated and distanced themselves from other students who were receiving special education services. Participants tried to demonstrate that they were similar to "normal" students, despite having IEPs. This desire to distinguish themselves from their peers may have contributed to the fraught peer relationships described in the previous section. Participants' wariness toward peers with IEPs reflects a common assumption that peers without IEPs are the "gold standard" for friendships and a prize for students with IEPs who are placed in general education classrooms. Unfortunately, this assumption ignores ways in which friendships with peers who also have IEPs can help students receiving special education services navigate the stigma of having a disability label and connect with others across shared experiences (Salmon, 2013), not to mention the many wonderful things that kids with IEPs can bring to friendships with peers without IEPs. The bias against friendships with students with disabilities were particularly challenging when students were spending part or all of their days in self-contained special education classes where all students had IEPs.

One student attempted to differentiate I from peers at a D75 school by explaining that the participant had previously attended a selective community school. When I asked why they had chosen to go to the selective school, this participant clarified, "the [selective] school choose me, cause I was good—I had good grades." On the other hand, this participant said that they had been forced to attend a D75 school because, "I got kicked out [of the previous school]. For fighting." This participant described school placements as reflections on student worth ("I was good") and behavior (having "good grades" or "fighting") rather than as places that were designed to develop students' unique strengths and meet their particular needs. As a result, this participant expressed wariness of other students at the D75 school, explaining that it was important to: "Not associate with people. Not get distracted. Just get my work done" in order to graduate.

Another participant who attended a co-located D75 school (a D75 school that shared a building with other "community" schools as part of a "campus" of secondary schools) introduced, and then immediately pushed back on the idea that students at that D75 school were different from other students in the building. This participant explained that students who attended other schools in the building, "think that, cause we in here, it's—that means that we crazy, or we slow or something." This participant pushes back on this belief, explaining, "But that don't mean that, that just means that we just learn, I mean, not really learn different, we just . . . some people probably learn different." Here, the student begins to challenge the idea that to "learn different" means to be "slow," reflecting a DS critique of the assumption that differences in how people learn are necessarily deficits (Gallagher, 2004). Ultimately, however, this participant also seemed to realize that "different" is not usually viewed positively in education, as they quickly qualified that most students at their school do "not really learn different," and that that the description only applies to "some people."

This participant further introduced the idea that there is a hierarchy of students within D75 schools, some of whom are more "different" than others. This participant explained, "it's kids with disability on this floor, but, that's that side—this this side. And this side is not the same as that side." In this euphemistic way, this student described the school's practice of separating students with different disability classifications and educating them in different parts of the building. This participant argued that while all students at the school were "kids with disability," the participant did not wish to be confused with students who they perceived to have an even lower status disability classification.

Similarly, another student differentiated I from peers with IEPs at a previous school that educated all students with IEPs in integrated co-taught classrooms with students without IEPs. When I asked that student for their opinion on this practice, they explained, "sometimes I get frustrated with the kids that do have a IEP, because they kind of slow up the work. But then I understand, because I did have an IEP." Despite having an IEP themselves, this participant's initial response was to differentiate and blame "the kids that do have an IEP" for slowing up the work.

BEING A TROUBLEMAKER VERSUS GETTING INTO TROUBLE

In presenting and explaining how peers served as both distractions and resources, participants also differentiated between a "type of kids" who gets into trouble (who I call "troublemakers"), and students who happened to get into trouble but were not necessarily the troublemaking "type." Participants sought to differentiate themselves from the perceived troublemakers, and expressed a desire to distance themselves from these students both physically and in others' minds. This differentiation occasionally seemed to benefit kids who were not perceived to be "troublemakers" when they got into trouble since getting into trouble was perceived to be out of character for them.

However, this perceived distinction between kids who *are* troublemakers and students who occasionally get into trouble may have contributed to participants viewing some peers with suspicion since participants, like my own students, described perceiving a porous border between the categories "troublemaker" and "students with IEPs." For example, two participants equated attendance at a D75 with "getting kicked out" of other schools, and one described peers at a D75 school as being there because of their "attitudes." This conflation of being a troublemaker with attending a D75 school may have further isolated students at those schools who wanted to avoid associating with peers they perceived to be risky.

One participant explained that school staff contributed to their understanding that some students were the "type of kids to just start trouble," while other students were not that "type," even if those students got into trouble occasionally. This student explained: "Everybody was cool with me, cause even when I was like, bad and I got suspended, they were cool with me because they knew I wasn't, like, the type of kids to just start trouble or something. Like, why you up here? You know you not supposed to be here." This student acknowledged having gotten into trouble and getting suspended, but asserted that they were not a troublemaking "type" of student. This participant described finding these two categories of students helpful, particularly because this student was positioned, and positioned themself, as someone who was not a troublemaker, even when they did get into trouble.

Another participant also differentiated between students at their D75 school who were troublemakers and those who were not, but suggested that the dividing line between troublemakers and other students was blurred in their mind. This participant explained, "this is a great school. It's just, you gonna be dealing with a whole bunch a different kids and the different attitudes," explaining further that some kids would give teachers a hard time. When asked what advice they would give a new teacher at the school, this participant said, "you can't be, like, soft on them, cause they gonna wanna push over on you. Cause they think, cause they here they got—you know, they being labeled as this, so they gonna act like that. No, you not gonna." This participant was one of the few to talk directly about how labeling might affect students negatively. As a result, this participant suggested that firm but empathetic teacher intervention could turn bad behavior into more positive behavior ("you not gonna" behave poorly).

A third student wrestled with answering the question "What are the kids [at your school] like?" At first, the participant described peers as, "athletic, energetic, reckless, stupid," introducing a range of positive and negative descriptions. When asked to elaborate, this student explained, "They like to do dumb stuff . . . hey, let's go steal something from a store, you know. Reckless stuff, you know," then qualified the statement saying "Got some kids like that, but, not all." This participant qualified the negative descriptions by limiting them to "some kids." This qualification also introduced the idea that there are different types of students at this school, representing a hierarchy with "some kids" who "do dumb stuff" positioned as "reckless" and even "stupid."

DISCUSSION

Across interviews, participants expressed complex and occasionally contradictory evaluations of their schools, staff, and peers differentiating between how particular policies and practices *should* and *did* affect them. Rather than drawing straight lines between a school-level factor and its perceived effect on themselves, participants considered whether school staff's actions aligned with their perceptions of what they imagined general education teachers do—focus on academic support, not behavior management or even social and emotional supports. In talking about peers as well, participants expressed concern that some of their classmates, particularly those with IEPs, posed risk to them. For students who attended D75 schools where all students had IEPs, that could lead to a very lonely school experience.

Disconnects between actions that adults intend to help students and how students perceive those actions must also be addressed. For example, many adults intend "special" education services to help students; however, none of the high school students I interviewed for this study, nor any middle or high school student I taught, ever expressed appreciation for and happiness about receiving special education services. Instead, they described navigating stigma and biases associated with being labeled and classified as having an "educational disability." At the very least, adults can expect resistance from students when they do not see our actions as being in their best interests. In general, though, we should carefully consider whether policies and practices that are not perceived as helpful by the people they are supposed to benefit are really worth continuing unaltered.

Chapter 5

Moving from the General to the Particular and Back

Generalizability and Variability in the School-to-Prison Pipeline

"They didn't prepare me because I never went . . . But they prepared the kids though."—Young participant expressing differences between their particular experience at a school and how they evaluated the school overall

Research on the school-to-prison pipeline (STPP) tends to be quantitative, looking at trends across larger groups. This research is important for guiding large-scale decisions, like which districts or schools need more resources and support. However, no single district, school, or even classroom is totally homogenous. Qualitative research helps policy makers and teachers better understand the diversity and variability across kids' experiences with schools. Qualitative research also helps us understand a topic in detail, and suggests new variables for further quantitative research. This chapter considers ways in which moving between a large-scale, administrative data set and individual interviews with kids can help policy makers and educators make sense of how the STPP affects different students, and also what might cause different kids to have different experiences, even within the same demographic categories. Further, this chapter addresses areas of convergence and divergence between directly or indirectly risky school-level factors identified by research and how participants talked about those school policies and practices.

In the quote that opens this chapter, a participant differentiates between their school helping "the kids" and the school actually helping them. When I first asked, "Did [your school] prepare you for the Regents?" (the New York State examinations required for high school graduation) the participant simply said, "Yeah." When I followed up and asked how, the student issued that clarification. Even after I pushed back a bit, saying, "Well, if they prepared the other kids and not you, and you're a student, then it doesn't sound like they did as good a job as they could have," the student simply repeated, "I mean, I wasn't going to school, so. They couldn't help me regardless. But I know they prepared for the Regents though." This brief interaction illustrates ways in which a school might do well with some students, but not others, as well as ways in which students often get blamed for mismatches between schools and kids.

Using a range of research methods to better understand the full complexity of kids' experiences with schools is important because current laws encourage or require schools to use "research-based" or "scientifically-based" knowledge to inform decisions. Unfortunately, this sensible recommendation often flattens "research" and "science" into exclusively quantitative research, which can suggest averages and modes, but does not, by itself, have much to say about any outliers. Students who are referred for special education services are usually, by definition, outliers—they are often the ones whom existing school policies and practices don't yet fit. As a result, it's particularly important to ensure that research intended to help students receiving special education services is capable of considering the diversity that exists in responding to any pedagogical approach, method, or strategy. This chapter will address some areas of convergence and divergence between the quantitative and qualitative strands of the study I conducted, as well as how my study built upon or contradicted the existing research base.

AREAS OF CONVERGENCE

This section addresses three areas of convergence between the quantitative and qualitative findings: (1) the relationship between student absences and arrest; (2) the relationship between suspensions and arrest; and (3) the relationships between standardized tests and arrest.

The Relationship between Attendance and Arrest

Regression analysis suggested that the average number of days students were absent in one year in New York City (NYC) secondary schools significantly predicted an increased likelihood that students with individualized education programs (IEPs) at that school had been arrested that year. In interviews, two students talked about cutting school, or cutting individual classes, and noted that missing class made academic success in that class extremely difficult. In addition, both students connected cutting school to a lack of relationships between that student and their teachers and peers, suggesting that cutting may be a symptom of other problems as well as a cause. In schools with high absence rates, even a student who does attend school regularly may find it difficult to make friends with peers whose presences are irregular and unpredictable. Although the quantitative data do not indicate whether individuals with high absence rates were the ones most likely to be arrested, interviews suggested that high schoolwide absence rates may negatively affect some students by making it difficult to form and maintain relationships among a transient student body. In addition, this finding builds upon a body of existing research correlating truancy with a variety of negative outcomes, such as leaving school before graduation, and linking truancy with the STPP (Rocque et al., 2017).

NYC has implemented several initiatives to increase student attendance in schools, such as texting families when students are absent (Singer, 2016), or even truancy court (Glaberson, 2010). However, these approaches generally focus on truancy as the cause of other problems rather than as a response to problems at school that may need to be addressed to make students feel safe and comfortable returning. Existing approaches to truancy also do not necessarily address the ways in which participants in this study described how missing school becomes a vicious circle, in which days absent lead to falling behind in work and a lack of friends, while feeling overwhelmed by missing schoolwork and not having friends served as disincentives to coming back to school. Participants in this study described being more motivated to come to school when there were people at school whom participants looked forward to seeing. One participant also described appreciating a teacher who did some of the work for them on a particular project, helping the participant complete the rest of the project by themself rather than allowing the participant to get overwhelmed and avoid doing any work on the project.

One participant even described a way in which their school's initiative to increase learning time had the opposite effect on them; this participant explained that their charter school's extended day was too long and tiring, so the participant said that they either left the school at lunch or avoided going altogether. This school's website advertises "more time to learn" through both extended school days and an extended school year, noting that students who attended the charter school from kindergarten through twelfth grade would have been exposed to six more years of "additional educational time" than students in traditional public schools. However, for at least one student, the extended days were counterproductive, leading to less instructional time as this participant simply avoided school. This participant explained that the school day "was just too long—I didn't want to be in school for that long . . . [the school] start at 8 a.m. and they end at 4 p.m. I wasn't staying there all day. So I would just go in the morning, and leave early, or I just don't go." This student suggested that, instead, "They could change the time from 8 a.m. to like one o'clock, 12:30 p.m. or something. Yeah. Other than that? That's it. That's the only problem I really have with this school." It is possible that the school days were simply too long, but it's also possible that the school could have incorporated more breaks and variety throughout the day to make a longer day more tolerable.

The Relationship between Suspension and Arrest

Quantitative models in this study suggested that the total percent of students in a school who have been suspended significantly increases the likelihood that a school will have students with IEPs who have been arrested. This result builds upon existing research suggesting that suspensions and expulsions are common but counterproductive responses to student misbehavior (e.g., Fabelo et al., 2011) that increase student misbehavior (Achilles et al., 2007; Skiba, 2002) and decrease the amount of instructional time made available to young people (Gregory et al., 2010). In addition, suspensions perpetuate inequitable opportunities offered to students based on race; Black students are disproportionately more likely to experience exclusionary punishments despite not exhibiting more or more severe behavioral infractions, meaning that Black students are given fewer opportunities to learn in school (e.g., Rocque & Paternoster, 2011).

Across interviews, every student named suspensions first as the response to students breaking school rules. This study cannot establish a specific causal link between suspensions and arrest; however, this study does suggest that suspensions interfered with participants' abilities to complete academic work and to form and maintain relationships with peers and adults at school. Although most students initially described suspensions as a fair response to student misbehavior, participants also noted that suspensions took students out of the classroom, making it difficult to complete work. In addition, suspensions contributed to two participants describing a lack of trust between themselves and their teachers. Participants described valuing adults who took time to get to know students and advise them based on the particular challenges which students might be facing at any time. On the other hand, suspensions are formal processes that involve administrators and families, rather than direct problem solving between adults and young people.

Because participants all suggested that schools' main purpose is to provide academic support to students, participants described rejecting rules that did not seem to be explicitly connected to academic achievement. Further, participants suggested alternatives to exclusionary punishments that prevented them from completing schoolwork. For example, one student suggested that an alternative to getting suspended for cutting class might be to make up missing work. This suggestion has the potential to appear more legitimate to students (since it supports, rather than detracts from, their learning) and also aligns better with schools' educative missions.

The Relationship between Standardized Tests and Arrest

One surprising result in statistical models was that schools with higher percentages of students passing English language arts (ELA) standardized tests were also more likely to be schools where students with IEPs had been arrested. A less surprising quantitative finding was that schools with higher percentages of students passing math standardized tests were less likely to be schools where students with IEPs had been arrested. Although standardized tests are often used as proxies for academic rigor in quantitative research, standardized tests have also been criticized for being racially biased (e.g., Nelson-Barber & Trumbull, 2007) and for having unintended consequences, such as pushing low-performing students out of school before graduation (e.g., Horn, 2003). As a result, high test scores may reflect schools "gaming the system," such as by excluding low-performing students, rather than a rigorous and engaging curriculum (Amrein-Beardsley, 2009). These efforts to game the system may explain the relationship between higher ELA pass rates and predicting YesArrest schools, although more research is needed. This study certainly suggests that the relationship between standardized tests scores and arrest is complex.

Participants also differentiated between math and ELA in talking about school, so it is possible that this surprising finding is related to differences between the math and ELA curricula in some NYC public schools. Three participants named math as their favorite subject; none named ELA. Three participants further said that they did not like reading and/or writing, which are two common activities in ELA courses. In addition, test pass rates were calculated using all students in a particular school who took a test, not only students with IEPs. The surprising finding about ELA scores may represent disparate opportunities offered to students with and without IEPs.

Another important distinction between Math and ELA tests is that the high school ELA test, the English Regents, is generally taken in eleventh grade, while the high school math test used in this study, the Algebra 1 Regents, is generally taken in ninth or even eighth grade. New York State offers other high school math exams as well, such as Algebra 2 and Geometry, but only students who are doing very well in math, or who attend particularly rigorous schools, take these optional math exams, making it difficult to interpret results and compare schools using this measure. As a result, this study only used Algebra 1 scores for high school math, since almost all students take them (unless those students attend one of the 28 consortium schools that are exempt, or the students participate in the New York State Alternate Assessment as indicated on their IEPs). Almost all students take the Algebra 1 Regents at least once; however, by eleventh grade, students are old enough to drop out, meaning that many students never take the English Regents.

AREAS OF DIVERGENCE

This section addresses two areas of divergence between quantitative and qualitative findings: (1) the relationship between school climate survey scores and arrest; and (2) the relationship between school age and arrest. This section also addresses the following two areas of divergence between my study's findings and the existing research: (1) the relationship between police in schools and arrest; (2) the relationship between discrimination and arrest.

The Relationship between School Climate and Arrest

Another surprising quantitative finding was that higher average school climate survey scores on questions related to student engagement predicted an increased likelihood that students with IEPs at that school will have been arrested. Across interviews, on the other hand, the majority (six) of participants described valuing teachers who made classes fun and engaging (with the exception of one student who named getting "respect" from teachers as most helpful).

Based on existing research, it is unlikely that increased engagement among students leads to arrest, since increased engagement has been correlated primarily with positive outcomes, such as academic performance (Smalls et al., 2007), while decreased engagement has been correlated with negative outcomes such as skipping school (Fallis & Opotow, 2003) and being pushed out of school (Christle et al., 2007; Smyth, 2007). One possible reason that school climate scores on questions related to student engagement may predict an increased likelihood that students with IEPs at that school will have been arrested may be that students with and without IEPs at many schools are offered different educational experiences and opportunities; for example, students with IEPs may be tracked into separate classes that are less engaging than what is offered to students without IEPs. Participants in my study were highly attuned to any ways in which their experiences as students with IEPs different from "regular" school experiences, so students at schools that offer very different opportunities to kids with and without IEPs may pose a greater risk to students with IEPs than schools that offer a more uniformly mediocre experience to all students. More research is necessary to consider why some students at positively-rated schools may still experience negative outcomes.

The Relationship between School Age and Arrest

Quantitative findings suggest that older schools (i.e., schools that have been in operation since before 2001, when federal and district policies led to many schools being closed and replaced) are more likely to be schools where students with IEPs have been arrested than newer schools. However, all but two of the schools described in interviews were newer schools that had opened since 2001. Between 2000 and 2014, the NYCDOE phased out, or began phasing out, 59 high schools that had low test scores, or over one-third of the 170 public high schools that existed in 1999 (Kemple, 2015). Among public secondary schools in NYC represented in this study, the majority (54.7 percent) have opened since 2001. This number does not represent schools that have opened after 2001, but closed before 2013, which is the beginning of the academic year for which this study uses data. One participant in this study attended a middle school that had both opened and closed since 2001. In other words, it is unsurprising that most interview participants had attended at least one newer school.

Regardless, the quantitative model that included school age was a poor overall fit for the data, making findings difficult to interpret, even though the school age variable was significant. As a result, it is difficult to make a claim about the relationship between school age and arrest in NYC based on this study.

The Relationship between Police in Schools and Arrest

Although research suggests that placing police officers in school is a directly risky policy, none of the high school students I spoke with described any negative encounters with police or security officers at their schools (they weren't always sure which was which). Each described school safety as being generally "nice," "friendly," or "aiight." At the same time, nobody described any particularly positive encounters or relationships with police officers or security guards that supported them in any ways.

Two participants argued that it was important to have police officers present in schools to protect students, with both mentioning concerns about school shootings. For example, one explained, "they have no metal detectors here. So, God forbid somebody bring a gun in, they [the police] could protect us." Another, similarly, argued that schools needed police officers, "Cause, they're actually here to protect us. They could have somebody running to school—a crazy person with a gun, and try to shoot everybody. That's what they here for." In addition to worrying about outside shooters, this student further expressed concerns about classmates, claiming, "all these kids want to fight, or somebody want to bring in a weapon." Although keeping kids safe is frequently the justification that is used for placing police officers in schools, and may be what these young people had heard, research suggests that schools remain the safest places for kids, and that police officers in schools like the ones these participants attended are more likely to arrest students than protect them from outside threats.

On the other hand, two participants argued that schools needed security guards but not necessarily police officers. For example, one said, "I don't think police officers [are necessary], but I think security guard—I mean, I don't know. It depends on what kind of school it is, I guess. If it's not like a school known for like having it bad there, then I guess . . . " Another explained, "I don't think it's that serious to have a whole police officer. A security guard, yes. I understand. It's gonna be fights. But, a police officer? . . . Nah . . . Cause, a security guard, they probably put you in handcuffs for a minute. But a whole police officer probably gonna take you back to the station." This student recognized that police officers had powers beyond what school staff normally had and argued that police officer's powers were more than what schools needed, even to break up fights.

In light of existing research suggesting that police officers in schools are a risk factor in the STPP, the lack of negative encounters with school police officers is encouraging, but the lack of genuinely positive or supportive encounters or relationships suggests that this study does not contradict the existing research that police officers in schools may cause more harm than good.

The Relationship between Discrimination and Arrest

One finding that surprised me was that each participant claimed that their schools generally treated kids fairly and equally based on their race, gender, sexual orientation, religion, and language spoken. For example, when I asked one participant to tell me about the kids in their school, the participant replied, "It's different groups. Different races. Different ages. All looking for—I think, I think all of us are looking for the same thing, cause we going to [a Specialized] School, so, most of them want to be [in the field of study that school focuses on]" and further explained that kids of "different races" hang out together regularly.

Although it would be nice to believe that participants attended utopian schools, free of discrimination of any sort, that seems unlikely. Because many participants did not know me well, they may have felt uncomfortable talking about sensitive topics like race and racism with me. As described further in Appendix B, I had hoped to build more of a relationship with participants in the study, but constraints around working with "vulnerable populations" made that difficult with the majority of participants. One participant suggested as much over the course of an interview. For example, when I asked one student, "Did you ever feel like you had any problems at your school because of your race or ethnicity?" the participant replied, "Not really, no. I don't know. Maybe. Sometimes. I don't—I don't know . . . Just, sometimes, like, the teachers—I don't know." However, when I asked this student if they would be willing to tell me more, the student replied, "I guess I'm gonna pass."

Two additional participants suggested that their schools weren't always as free of discrimination as they initially claimed. One participant also first simply answered, "No," when I asked, "did—do you know if kids ever had any problems with like, kids from other racial groups? Or ethnic groups?" However, when I followed up, asking, "Did people ever, like, call each other names, or get into fights, or, people got along?" the student replied, "Oh, yeah! Racial slurs. Yeah." This response made me wonder how the student had originally interpreted my question and how I might have worded it differently so that the student wasn't surprised ("Oh, yeah!") when they realized what I was asking.

A third participant similarly changed their initial responses that discrimination wasn't a problem to say, "it was more like—one teacher. I think she didn't mean it, but, she said something real racist. I said, what? I said, that's pretty racist, you know. But. She said, oh really? Mmmm, yeah!" It's possible that the participant didn't feel like one racist incident was worth discussing, or possible that the participant thought the incident had been resolved—it's wonderful that the participant was able to push back on what the teacher had said. However, this student may have also been reluctant to discuss the incident with me further, claiming that they "forgot" what the teacher had said, but that, "I know most of the people I had in my class remember it." It's possible, but seems unlikely, that the student really couldn't give any more description of what the teacher had said if "most of the people" in their class would have remembered this incident.

Although participants consistently expressed the belief that there was no discrimination at their schools (at least initially), two participants expressed some homophobia themselves. For example, when I asked one participant if they thought kids ever got treated differently because of their sexual orientation, they responded, "Maybe," and followed up saying that they knew kids who identified as gay and lesbian, "But I stay away . . . I don't know. I say whassup. That's it. I don't try to make conversation . . . I just don't want to get involved . . . No parts" (the ellipses represent both long pauses in the conversation and places where I continued to probe the student's responses). Another said more bluntly, "I don't like gay people. I'm sorry. I—I'm not gonna say it to they face, but I wouldn't let nobody who's gay near me." Both participants suggest some recognition that homophobia might be frowned upon (e.g., "I'm sorry") but also wanted to be clear that they held homophobic beliefs themselves. This study suggests that schools need to do more and do better to protect students from homophobia.

DISCUSSION

The results of any single study are just that—one set of findings. However, the ways in which this study's findings converge or diverge with existing research can help build upon existing ideas about how best to divert the STPP or suggest new areas of complexity and diversity among students' experiences. The final chapter will offer some concrete suggestions for diverting the STPP.

Chapter 6

Diverting the School-to-Prison Pipeline

"At all my other schools, I used to like, get kicked out of everything. I don't even remember all the names of the schools . . . [At the most recent school I attended], they made us feel like it was home. They made us, like, if you don't have a mother, there was a mother here. Or, a grandmother, or a aunt, a uncle, a dad . . . I don't think I woulda really changed anything because to me, like, the school was actually a good school."—Participant explaining how a school finally supported them

Diversity is normal. In any group of students, no matter how "homogeneous" the grouping, there will be kids with different interests, strengths, preferences, and needs for support. Educators have three choices when confronting this diversity: (1) try to reduce it as much as possible; (2) accept it and teach different kids in different ways; or (3) leverage that diversity to enhance everyone's learning. Historically and currently, schools often focus on the first choice, then use the second choice when they are unable to follow through with the first. However, research suggests that all kids benefit when we treat diversity as a valuable educational tool that can enhance the learning of all students (from both majoritized and minoritized groups). This chapter will suggest ways to do so.

A note—a lot of educational research uses "diverse" as a euphemism to refer to homogenous groups of kids who are from a minoritized group. However, a group consisting only of Spanish speakers is no more (or less) diverse than a group consisting only of English speakers. A group consisting of *both* Spanish and English speakers has more linguistic diversity, but many New York City classrooms have students speaking a wide range of languages (e.g., Spanish and English, *and* also Mandarin, Arabic, Russian, Urdu, etc.) When I talk about diversity throughout the book, I am referring to this diversity—to kids who are different from each other in a variety of ways, leaning from and with each other, in the same place.

Although more and more people are coming to recognize that a diverse group of peers and teachers is, by itself, an important educational resource, many people still seem to think that diversity of dis/ability is still a liability rather than an asset. Many people who think racially segregated schools are appalling still think it's a good idea to educate kids with disabilities in separate settings from their peers without disabilities. Further, many people assume that students with disabilities are the primary beneficiaries of inclusive classrooms in which students with and without individualized education programs (IEPs) learn together, rather than recognizing ways in which able-bodied, neurotypical kids benefit both from learning from their peers with who do and think about things differently from them, and also from being in classrooms that are designed to teach the diverse range of abilities that is present in any group of humans.

In this chapter, I make suggestions for both practitioners and policy makers about ways to better support diverse students and divert the school-to-prison pipeline (STPP) for students with (and without) IEPs. Some of the suggestions for educators will be difficult to enact within the current policy climate. Nevertheless, educators can look for opportunities to "teach against the grain" (Cochran-Smith, 1991) and act to help the young people in their care, even when existing policy encourages practices that may be harmful to young people receiving special education services. Schools cannot—and should not be expected to—solve all of the many problems that lead kids to wind up in prisons and jails. But, at the very least, we should expect schools to cause no additional harm to students. The STPP is one way in which schools harm some students and, as a result, is within the power and responsibility of education policy and practice to change.

In keeping with young people's insistence that schools should first and foremost support academic learning, this chapter first suggests some approaches to academic instruction that use diversity as an educational asset rather than seeing it as a liability. Next, I'll suggest some approaches to creating a positive, nurturing school climate for middle and high school students that are aligned with school's educative purposes and less likely to cause harm to children with (and without) IEPs, such as moving them through the STPP. Finally, this chapter acknowledges some things that we still don't fully understand about the STPP that should be addressed by future research.

ACADEMIC SUPPORT FOR AND FROM DIVERSE STUDENTS

Diversity in schools is frequently framed as a problem that needs to be solved rather than as an opportunity for learning. This is particularly true in schools and classes that educate students with diverse abilities, from diverse racial and ethnic backgrounds, and who speak diverse languages. As a result, this section offers suggestions for teaching kids who are diverse along these particular axes together, within the same classroom, in ways that capitalize upon the many advantages of diversity to enhance everyone's learning. Research suggests that learning from and with diverse classmates has many benefits for all students' learning as they are exposed to and learning about different ways of being, doing, and thinking about various topics and issues.

I will briefly address three promising approaches for making rigorous curriculum accessible to all and for leveraging the diverse funds of knowledge that a diverse group of students will bring to a classroom: Universal Design for Learning (UDL), culturally relevant teaching (CRT), and multilingual education. Research suggests that "cross-pollinating" (Waitoller & Thorius, 2016) across these approaches can lead to even better outcomes than using each in isolation. Unfortunately, teacher preparation programs and in-service professional development for teachers do not always adequately prepare teachers for working with diverse learners; pre- and in-service teachers will likely need support to implement these approaches.

Universal Design for Learning

UDL comes from the concept of "universal design" in architecture. Something is universally designed when it can be used by everyone. For example, a ramp is universally designed because it can be used by anyone who needs to ascend or descend, whether that person is walking or wheeling. A ramp is necessary for some—particularly those who are on wheels—but beneficial for many more, such as those who are pushing strollers, pulling suitcases, or walking bikes. On the other hand, stairs are not universally designed since they cannot be used by many people (e.g., people who use wheelchairs).

Within education, the curriculum is universally designed when all students can participate and benefit (CAST, 2020). Designing curriculum meant to be meaningful and accessible to all students from the beginning contrasts with the more traditional way of designing curriculum with the expectation that all students will participate and benefit in the same way, then adding additional access points or accommodations for only some students.

For example, a science teacher using a traditional approach might ask students to read a chapter about the circulatory system in the textbook, then answer the questions at the back of the chapter. After consulting students' IEPs, the teacher might have a paraprofessional read the chapter aloud to one student, and allow a second student to dictate responses into an audio recorder rather than writing the responses by hand. However, most students would complete the assignment the same way: by reading the printed text, then using a pen or pencil to write responses.

Just as a ramp benefits many people who don't strictly need it, many "accommodations" that are necessary for some will benefit many students who don't strictly need them. For example, research suggests that reading aloud to students (including middle and high school students) helps build fluency and improve their pronunciation of academic vocabulary in addition to improving comprehension among many students. Why restrict the opportunity to hear a news article read aloud to one student when more would benefit? Further, requiring all students to write what they know about the circulatory system risks invalidating assessment results for students who do poorly—was the problem that the student really didn't understand the difference between arteries and veins, or is the real problem that the student doesn't yet have the writing skills to explain that difference in this format?

With that in mind, a teacher using UDL would try to find as many ways to represent information, allow students to participate in learning activities, and assess student learning as possible knowing that "accommodations" that are necessary for some students would likely benefit many more. For example, students might learn about the circulatory system by using and producing printed texts (like textbooks and scientific research articles), podcasts, video clips, diagrams, and three-dimensional models. When students have choices about how to represent their learning, it is also easier to interpret and act upon assessment data. For example, the student whose written description of the difference between arteries and veins was unclear might draw a diagram using blue for veins, and arrows showing blood flowing back to the heart, and red for arteries, with arrows showing blood flowing away from the heart. Adding this diagram to the ix would make clear that the student does, indeed, understand the concept but may need support with expressing ideas in writing.

UDL shows promise for use in genuinely inclusive classes that provide students with a range of abilities access to a rigorous curriculum using multiple access points. Inclusive classes have many benefits for kids with and without IEPs. The interviews I conducted with high school students build upon over a century of research and anecdotal evidence that separate, segregated classes for students who are perceived to have disabilities have never been equal in the United States, and may never be viewed as legitimate by students, teachers, and other stakeholders. While some argue that we could enhance instructional quality while maintaining two separate systems, the fact that we have not found a way to make these two separate systems equal in either quality or legitimacy since their inception over a century ago suggests that other goals, like unifying the system, may be worth considering instead. UDL is one approach that can support diverse students' academic achievement in a unified system.

Culturally Relevant, Responsive, and Sustaining Pedagogies

Although it is no longer legal to use race as the rationale for segregating students and giving them access to unequal educational opportunities, these practices still occur throughout the United States, with NYC maintaining one of the most racially segregated school systems in the country. Racial diversity is still often framed as a problem that needs to be solved, that makes teachers' work more difficult than teaching in a racially homogeneous school would be. However, culturally relevant (Ladson-Billings, 1995, 2014), responsive (Gay, 2010), and sustaining pedagogies (Paris & Alim, 2012), as well as other related approaches such as culturally congruent teaching or multicultural education use racial and ethnic diversity as a learning opportunity rather than viewing it as a problem. Although there are important differences among the approaches described by those terms, there are many similarities as well. When I teach graduate students who are learning to be special educators, I usually use the term "culturally relevant teaching" and focus on the three tenets that Ladson-Billings (1995) first identified: academic achievement, cultural competence, and sociopolitical awareness. Academic achievement is, of course, the main goal of every approach to teaching. The development of cultural competence involves gaining a deeper, positive understanding of one's own cultural groups and background. Sociopolitical awareness requires kids to understand larger social and political issues and problems, such as ableism, racism, and poverty.

Many researchers and practitioners currently recommend CRT as a way to reduce disproportional representation within special education. Disproportional representation refers to kids from different racial and ethnic backgrounds not being distributed across disability classifications and settings in the ratios we would expect based on how they are represented in the population at large. For example, the percent of Black students in segregated special education classrooms and schools is much higher than the percent of Black students in particular districts (this is a pattern that is true across the country, although the exact ratios vary slightly from district to district). CRT has also been suggested as an approach to reduce the disproportionate representation of kids from different racial and ethnic groups along the STPP. Although disproportionality is a clear indicator of persistent racism in schools, researchers and educators disagree about whether the problem will be solved when all racial and ethnic groups are proportionally represented across special education settings and throughout the STPP or whether a more radical solution (e.g., abolishing segregated special education settings entirely) may be required to improve educational outcomes for racially and ethnically diverse students (again, I am using the term "diverse" not just to refer to racially and ethnically minoritized groups but also to White students, who are harmed in different ways by racist policies and practices).

Building upon the Universally Designed unit on the circulatory system described in the previous system, a culturally relevant science educator might build students' cultural competence (and academic achievement) by incorporating research on the circulatory system from all over the world (not just from White and European scientists), and by suggesting ways to develop and maintain cardiovascular health using physical activity from multiple places and cultures (e.g., dances and adaptive dance from different countries and cultures or sports and adaptive sports from all over the world) and eating healthy foods from a range of different cuisines. This teacher could build students' sociopolitical awareness (and academic achievement) but addressing public health disparities related to cardiovascular disease, and the ways in which those public health disparities relate to other disparities related to food access, environmental inequalities, and biases within the healthcare system.

Disproportional representation of kids from different racial and ethnic groups in both special education and the STPP is a symptom of the education debt (Ladson-Billings, 2006) that the United States owes to kids whose communities have historically not been given equal educational opportunities and who are still not being given equal educational opportunities. Although a lot needs to be done at the policy level to provide a more equitable distribution of resources (more on that shortly), CRT is one approach that teachers can use within their classrooms to begin disrupting enduring inequalities among students from different racial, ethnic, and linguistic groups.

Multilingual Education

Although speaking multiple languages has always seemed to me to be obviously better than speaking one language, U.S. education policy and practice have historically promoted, and continue to promote, monolingualism rather than multilingualism—a practice that Valenzuela (1999) has referred to as "subtractive schooling," in which schools attempt to remove rather than add to students' knowledge. Many existing policies and practices do not even meet that strange but stated goal, though. For example, "English only" policies and practices for kids who speak languages other than English at home do not support students' English acquisition as well as policies and practices that draw upon multilingual students' full linguistic repertoires.

There is currently debate within special education about whether kids are being incorrectly classified as having disabilities when "English only" and other discredited policies and practices fail many of them. Some argue that many kids who are new to English and who are given IEPs don't "really" have disabilities and, as a result, should not be receiving "special" education services for students with disabilities but, rather, should be receiving special services for English learners. However, as I've argued elsewhere in this book, a more relevant question might be to ask how schools can better enable all kids, including multilingual learners, to learn and succeed, rather than on focusing on identifying which kids "really" have a disability. Approaches like UDL and CRT can support students with and without IEPs, and who speak a variety of languages at home.

Multilingual education shows the most promise both for developing multilingual citizens in general and for developing English proficiency among students who speak other languages at home in particular. Multilingual education can refer to a range of practice that draw upon and develop students' proficiency in multiple (at least two) languages. For example, some schools in NYC (and other places) offer two-way immersion bilingual programs. Kids who speak two different languages—say, English and Korean—at home learn together in the same classroom using both languages, taught by either a bilingual teacher or by two teachers who each use one of the languages (e.g., one teacher who teaches in English and a second who teaches in Korean). This approach can lead to all students developing bilingual proficiency, whether they start school speaking English or Korean (or even multilingual proficiency among students enrolled in the bilingual class who speak a third language at home).

Even in English-dominant classrooms, approaches like translanguaging support students' full linguistic repertoire as they draw upon multiple languages throughout the school day. For example, the science teacher who is beginning the unit on the circulatory system might add resources in multiple languages, and allow students to use multiple languages to participate in activities. Even if the science teacher is monolingual, the teacher can find and add printed texts, video clips, and other resources in multiple languages for students to use. The teacher can also encourage students to use whichever language is most comfortable for them when they are working in groups, brainstorming, journaling, etc. There may certainly be times when particularly assignments will be submitted in English, but many of the preplanning and prewriting stages would not need to be conducted in English.

As part of a culturally relevant education, teachers should develop students' sociopolitical awareness around which languages and dialects are privileged in particular situations. Just as a suit is sometimes expected by others in certain situations, some dialects of English are considered more "formal" or "standard" and kids need to learn them. Kids should also learn that there is nothing better (i.e., more sophisticated or more capable of communicating ideas) about any particular dialect any more than a suit is "better" clothing than sweats (I would personally argue that sweats are a "better" item of clothing since they are more functional for a range of activities, but I do know that wearing sweats to most types of job interviews would not work in my favor, unfortunately). Instead, ideas about which ways of speaking and dressing are most "appropriate" are linked to biases about the people who use them.

SCHOOL CLIMATE AND DISCIPLINE

Although academic achievement is the most important and distinctive purpose of schools, research suggests that school climate and disciplinary practices affect student learning and are closely connected to the STPP. As more and more research emerges showing ways in which exclusionary discipline is both counterproductive to its original goals and creates new, additional problems for students and schools, more schools and districts are moving away from suspensions and expulsions as the first response to disciplinary infractions. However, each high school student I spoke with named suspensions first when I asked them what happened if kids broke the rules at their schools. None of these participants attached any sort of educational purpose of value to suspensions. For example, when I asked one participant whether they thought suspensions were fair, they responded, "Do I think—mmm, honestly, I don't care what the consequence is. All I know is I just have to face it."

Some argue that removing disruptive students is worth the well-documented harm to those students if it gives other students a chance to learn; however, research suggests that an overreliance on suspensions and expulsions creates a negative school climate that makes it difficult for any student to learn, including the ones who remain in schools. The students I spoke with described ways in which missing school alienated them from peers and teachers, and also led to overwhelming amounts of work when they returned. Further, exclusionary disciplinary policies may hinder students' academic growth through diminishing the amount of instruction made available to students (Gregory et al., 2010). As a result, Warnick and Scribner (2020), among others, have pointed out that these "disciplinary practices are antithetical to the aims of schooling" (p. 8).

Although people can, and do, argue about what, exactly, we are trying to accomplish by building and maintaining a system of public education, many people would probably agree that the purpose of this system is to teach kids stuff—although people would also probably immediately start disagreeing about *what*, exactly, schools should teach or *how*, exactly, schools should teach it. Suspensions and expulsions don't necessarily teach students how to do things differently when different behaviors may be warranted.

At the most extreme end of exclusionary disciplinary policies, the presence of police officers across NYC schools—and in schools across the country—increase the likelihood that students will be arrested for normal, developmentally appropriate adolescent behavior such as talking back to adults or cutting class.

Arresting children is traumatic both for them and for their classmates (NYCLU, 2018). Particularly troubling are data indicating that 30.1 percent of school incidents involving police during the 2018–2019 involved children in emotional crisis who were brought to hospitals; 7.5 percent of these children were handcuffed (NYCLU, 2019a). The largest percent of police incidents end in "mitigation," meaning that 48 percent of students were released back to their schools during the 2018–2019 school-year (NYCLU, 2019a). These two categories, making up nearly 80 percent of police interventions, would clearly be better handled by trained mental health professionals and school staff such as teachers, administrators, and/or guidance counselors. Only three percent of these police incidents involved children being accused of committing felonies, representing an overall rate of 0.003 percent of public school students. In other words, given the extreme rarity of children being accused of committing serious crimes at school, the harms of keeping police officers stationed within schools outweigh the benefits.

On the other hand, other approaches to school discipline have shown more promise for both meeting their stated goals ("better," or at least more desirable behavior) and also for fulfilling the educative purpose of schools—equipping kids with the knowledge and skills they need to behave "better" and in ways that allow academic learning to flourish. The following sections suggest ways to promote a positive school climate that that fulfills schools' missions to educate students rather than relying on suspensions and expulsions.

Behavior Management: Punishments and Rewards

Although pure behaviorism, by itself, is not sufficient to help adolescent students develop into ethical adults, punishments and rewards can serve as helpful motivators at times. For example, as an adult, there are certain parts of my work I would probably not do if I didn't fear the threat of punishments (e.g., getting fired) or want the reward of a paycheck. It's probably also not reasonable to expect kids to find every single activity at school riveting and inherently motivating, although schools could certainly do a better job of developing and implementing engaging, relevant curriculum to reduce the reliance on punishments and rewards.

Although research suggests that rewards are more effective at changing behavior than punishments—more on that in a moment—as a teacher, I found that students were surprisingly receptive to punishments that were clearly connected to educational goals. Although some adults prefer to use the term "consequences" over "punishments," I was never fooled by that as a kid, nor were any of my students. Regardless, the nature of the punishment/consequence mattered more than what I called it. If the punishment/consequence was clearly connected to supporting student learning, then I got very little pushback (if any). For example, when students were goofing off in class and did not complete assigned work, I required them to come back to my classroom during lunch or after school to finish whatever work was missing. Sometimes students were annoyed when I first told them, but by the time they returned to my room with their work in hand, they usually offered no resistance. Some students even told me, seeming surprised, that this punishment seemed fair to them, especially compared to teachers who made them go to detentions where they engaged in pointless work that they would not earn credit for. Having been a student and a teacher, I think that minimal but strategic use of punishments can help adolescents understand where boundaries are. Just as the participants in my study were more likely to find disciplinary practices that were clearly aligned with academic goals to be more legitimate, Thompson et al. (2020) have argued that "schools act most legitimately in punishing students when they do so in reference to a legitimate educational license" (p. 8).

Although strategic use of punishments may be helpful in small doses, research and experience both suggest that it's best to give students clear expectations for what is expected and why, and then reward them for meeting expectations rather than just punishing them when they fail to live up to expectations. Approaches like Positive Behavioral Interventions and Supports or Culturally Relevant Positive Behavioral Interventions and Supports (even better) formalize that process, often with points and levels that students accumulate to earn rewards. This approach is promising and can be helpful for many students. However, as a caveat, I found mixed results with formal behavior programs as a teacher. Some of my students never earned enough points to "make level" and earn rewards. Some of these students might have a great week, then forget to bring in a note for an absence, meaning they lost all points for that day. Other students might have a great day or even class period in the middle of a week where they were not earning points at other times. It was discouraging to them to feel like a great day or class period didn't matter in the context of the larger week. As a result, even this approach that was intended to "catch kids doing well" seemed to emphasize all of the things that students had done wrong in some cases.

Of course, teachers can adapt or create their own systems of punishments and rewards that flexibly meet the needs of their students. Making sure that all rules and consequences are explicitly tied to academic achievement may help the rules and consequences appear more legitimate to students than rules and consequences that appear to be primarily about teachers establishing their own authority or acting tough. Just because a rule seems clearly aligned with academic achievement to an adult (e.g., not coming to school high) does not necessarily mean that the connection is readily apparent to adolescents, especially when the consequences for breaking that rule (e.g., getting sent home from school) are clearly making it difficult for students to be academically successful. Making sure that rewards and punishments are clearly linked to academic achievement may help maintain their legitimacy in the eyes of middle and high school students.

Teaching Kids to Do Better

Although behavioral management tools like punishments and rewards have their place, they work best when kids already know what they need to do and need a bit of motivation to get it done. As a result, other approaches are necessary to teach kids how to resolve interpersonal conflicts and address other complex problems. Research suggests that restorative justice practices show promise for positively altering students' behaviors and improving school climate (e.g., Anyon et al., 2016; Gregory et al., 2016; Stinchcomb et al., 2006).

One important aspect of restorative justice that is frequently cited in the existing research is that kids (and adults) must actually repair mistakes they have made rather than simply getting punished for them. For example, a student who vandalized a classroom would have to clean and re-paint the classroom rather than simply getting a detention. A student who insulted another child would have to have a conversation with the other child to find a way to make things right between them, and then follow up by doing whatever the pair agreed upon. A mediator would help facilitate these conversations to make sure that everyone's needs are met. Restorative justice helps kids learn how to solve problems, while punishments simply show the boundaries of "acceptable" behavior but don't necessarily offer alternative options.

Unfortunately, the high school students I spoke with who reported that their school engaged in restorative practices also noted that the results were uneven. For example, one participant said that sometimes, rather than suspending kids who were fighting, the school would "Try to calm them down, have a conflict resolution . . . have us talk to each other." This participant said that it was "sometimes" helpful, and explained, "one time, it was good— it worked out, [the other student and I] became good friends after that." However, this student argued that conflict resolution was not always successful: "I mean, if you can't do it, you can't do it, but they'd just try to force it, like, hey, hey, you should talk about it . . . Sometimes [students who are having problems] just want to fight again when they see each other." Conflict mediation and other restorative practices cannot be implemented as uniformly as some other approaches; they require a great deal of skill and support.

More Strategic Staffing Choices

As mentioned above, the vast majority of incidents involving police in schools are either referred back to school staff or end with children being transported to hospitals for mental health care. Only an extremely small minority of incidents involve children being accused of committing serious crimes. With that in mind, staffing should be adjusted to reflect kids' needs. The following recommendations build upon recent calls to ensure that problems that would best be addressed by mental health professionals, educators, and others with specific and relevant expertise are not all dumped on police officers who may be ill-prepared to work with children exhibiting either typical or worrisome behaviors. Of course, even if police officers were no longer employed by public schools, schools would still be able to call 911 in the extremely rare event that a serious crime were committed on campus and the school wished to request police assistance, just as any other citizen or institution might.

Currently, the NYC public schools employ approximately 5,200 school safety agents (NYCLU, 2019b) and less than 2,900 full-time guidance counselors (NYCDOE, 2019) across approximately 1,800 schools, which leads to a ratio of approximately one guidance counselor per 360 students, which is significantly higher than the American School Counselor Association's recommended ratio of 1 counselor per 250 students. New York City public schools could achieve this ratio with 4,400 guidance counselors. If all police officers employed by NYC schools were replaced by guidance counselors, the ratio would fall to 1 guidance counselor per 134 students. One high school student I spoke with gave me an example of how their guidance counselor built a relationship with them over time that allowed the counselor to help this student with a range of problems, explaining, "I don't really like talking to everybody. But, we'll talk. Most of the time, I'll be like, can we play Uno? And she'll be like, all right. That's how they would get me to talk . . . Instead of sitting here, just looking at each other face for a while." This counselor was able to gently break down this student's resistance to "talking to everybody" by playing games, which removed some of the intense pressure the student felt when they were "just looking at each other face." One reason that it's so important for student–counselor ratios to be lower than they are is that this type of skilled relationship building takes time that simply isn't available when a guidance counselor is responsible for advising 360 children.

Alternatively, after hiring an additional 1,400 guidance counselors to meet staffing recommendations, NYC public schools might consider hiring an additional 3,800 teachers to replace the remaining 3,800 police officers of the 5,200 currently employed by public schools. These teachers might be distributed evenly across the city, giving each school an additional two teachers, or might be targeted to schools with higher student–teacher ratios. Schools might employ additional teachers to reduce student–teacher ratios, allowing kids and adults to form closer, more positive relationships that improve school climate. Alternatively, additional teachers might bring new classes like art, music or advanced science courses that enrich the curriculum and increase kids' engagement with and attachment to their schools. Engagement is positively correlated with academic achievement (Smalls et al., 2007) and a variety of other positive outcomes such as graduation rates (Christle et al., 2007).

The American Civil Liberties Union (2019), among others, have also recommended replacing police officers stationed in schools with nurses, psychologists, and social workers, finding that 14 million students across the country were in schools with police but no counselor, nurse, psychologist, or social worker. These professionals would certainly be better prepared and suited to deal with children's emotional and mental health needs than police officers.

OTHER SCHOOL-LEVEL RECOMMENDATIONS

Academic achievement is the main goal of schools, and school discipline is a key factor in pushing kids along the STPP. However, this study, and existing research, also identify a few other school-level policies and practices that may interact with the STPP. When these and other school-level policies and practices are not clearly and explicitly linked to academic achievement, students might find those policies and practices to be illegitimate and those policies and practices may have negative effects.

For example, although all participants in this study had attended at least one school with a uniform policy, there is little research supporting uniforms' effectiveness in increasing student academic achievement (Viadero, 2005; Yeung, 2009). Two of four students in this study who attended schools with uniforms said that was one of the things they would change about their schools; no student said that the uniform policy was something they liked or found helpful in any way. Further, uniform policies can harm students who are punished or lose instructional time because their families could not afford to buy or launder uniforms. In the absence of any documented educational benefits (e.g., through improved achievement) and presence of documented harms (e.g., to students who skip school when their uniforms are dirty), there is no compelling case for keeping uniform policies in public schools.

Although, teachers and other school staff are under strict accountability and other pressures, participants in this study emphasized the importance of adults taking time to form and maintain relationships with students when possible. This finding builds upon existing research on how strong, positive teacher–student relationships support adolescents with IEPs emotionally and academically (e.g., Murray & Pianta, 2007). Although participants frequently described school rules and consequences that did not seem directly academic, such as dress codes and suspensions, to be unfair, participants also described themselves accepting guidance from adults who took a personal interest in them. For example, the participant who said that it was "just not the school's business" to address students coming to school high also said that they had "changed my mind about everything I was doing" since that time and wanted to decrease their substance use in general. This participant described talking to adults at school whom they had a more positive relationship with, such as the guidance counselor, about their drug use, noting that they "always wanted to talk to her" and found her to be helpful. This participant, and three others, seemed to differentiate between adults simply acting as caring adults and acting as official arms of the school. One thing that differentiated a caring adult was that caring adults did not engage in formalized processes with punishments, but offered individualized guidance and support related to specific situations students were in.

In addition, this study suggests that the practice of extending school days and years will not automatically increase student learning. One student argued that the extended school day at their charter school served as a disincentive to attend at all. Schools that have longer school days should take into account adolescent student's attention spans and stamina, and make sure that there are opportunities for breaks and a variety of activities over the course of the school day. However, it's also worth remembering that children are not machines—there is a point every day at which they will not be able to keep absorbing new information. If schools decide to extend their hours, they should carefully monitor the effects on students to see whether extended hours hit diminishing returns or even create additional problems for students.

RECOMMENDATIONS FOR POLICY

Policy's influence on practice is complex; research suggests that schools and educators may make sense of and enact policies in a variety of complex ways that do not always align with the policy's original goals (Bertrand & Marsh, 2015). However, policy can provide conditions which facilitate or hinder various educational practices, such as the ones I've recommended in this chapter. For example, many approaches to teaching diverse learners, like UDL, CRT, multilingual education, and restorative practices, require a great deal of skill and knowledge from teachers. Policy can support teachers' acquisition of the necessary skills and knowledge at the pre- and in-service level by requiring and funding teacher education that addresses these promising practices throughout teachers' careers.

One larger educational policy which should be reconsidered is the practice of segregating students with disabilities and educating them in separate settings from their peers without disabilities. Since the first days of mandatory, "common" schooling for children in the United States, young people with disabilities have been denied many of the rights their peers without disabilities enjoy (Richardson, 1994). Today, disability remains an acceptable excuse for giving some young people inferior educational opportunities, and for accepting inferior outcomes. Court cases have persistently limited schools' legal obligations toward students with IEPs (e.g., Board of Education of the Hendrick Hudson Central School District v. Rowley, 1982). In addition, policy permits the continued segregation of young people with IEPs if the IEP committee determines that the "least restrictive environment" suitable for those young people is a segregated setting (IDEA, 2004). The high school students I spoke with represented a range of special education placements, from "regular" classrooms to entirely segregated schools. However, participants who spoke about special education all addressed the stigma and perceived inferiority of the services they received, particularly when those services occurred in separate settings.

It was not inevitable that the United States would develop two separate educational systems, or prepare different sets of teachers, to educate young people with and without disabilities. For example, other countries use more flexible support systems in which kids can get help whenever they need it rather than waiting for a formal classification process to provide access to particular services like counseling or speech therapy. In addition to not separating and stigmatizing students, this flexible process allows students who are experiencing situational problems, such as the death of a parent, that would not qualify them for an IEP, to access help when they need it. A more flexible service delivery model in U.S. schools could benefit many young people who are not currently receiving special education services as well.

Special education as an institution, and the medical model of disability as a framework for thinking about educating kids with disabilities, has certainly made some valuable contributions to teaching and learning. However, there is usually no need to provide those services, approaches, methods, or strategies to only some students. Flexible, accessible teaching benefits students without identified disabilities as well as students receiving special education services. Students without disabilities are not a homogenous group; they also benefit from accessible curriculum. In the rare situations where only some students would benefit from a particular service (e.g., a hearing aid linked to a teacher microphone), those services can be provided in inclusive settings. In general, the strategies and supports that would benefit students with IEPs (e.g., making sure all important information is also presented visually to benefit students with hearing impairments) would also benefit students without IEPs (i.e., all students, with and without hearing impairments, benefit from having information presented using multiple modalities).

Policy's support for zero-tolerance disciplinary policies should also change. Zero-tolerance policies have become nearly ubiquitous across the United States since the Gun-Free Schools Act of 1994 (Eskenazi et al., 2003). However, research has documented many negative effects of these policies (e.g., missed class time, negative school climate). This study builds upon those findings, and suggests that schools with high suspension rates are also likely to be schools where at least one student with an IEP has been arrested.

This study builds upon others which suggest the importance of strong, caring relationships with both adults and peers in their schools through both the positive impacts of their presence and the negative effects of their absences. However, teachers face multiple and mounting accountability pressures that interfere with their abilities to form and maintain relationships with and across students (e.g., Stillman, 2011). As with all educators in the United States since 2001, educators in NYC are expected to produce higher test scores and engage with quantifiable data. However, this study builds upon others that suggest that high test scores and quantifiable data alone do not always mean that everything at a school is perfect, as schools with higher ELA test pass rates were also more likely to be schools in which students with IEPs had been arrested. Further, students with IEPs may face particularly negative relationships with educators when they are viewed as liabilities for potentially not earning high scores on high-stakes assessments. Just as punishments alone will not help students learn how to do better, accountability alone will not help teachers learn how to teach better. Support for teachers, such as professional development and adequate planning time will likely lead to better academic outcomes for their students with, and without, IEPs.

CONCLUSION

Research suggests that school policies and practices can increase the likelihood that young people receiving special education services will pass through the STPP. Although the criminal justice system in the United States is complex and in need of overhaul that cannot be accomplished by schools alone, we can certainly expect schools to avoid making problems worse. This chapter suggested ways in which schools can alter those factors that are within their control to reduce the number of children getting arrested and incarcerated.

More research is necessary to better understand the diverse ways in which kids with (and without) IEPs make sense of their time at school in general, and special education in particular. When the people who are supposed to benefit most from a particular service or institution don't find that service or institution valuable or helpful, it's worth considering why and what alternatives may be available. Diversity across many other categories (e.g., race, gender, language) is increasingly recognized as an asset within any classroom rather than a liability. I hope that diversity across dis/ability will be recognized and used as the asset it is as well, and that schools and teachers will continue to adapt to better serve diverse students and leverage those students' funds of knowledge to create better outcomes for all.

Appendix A

Who Benefits from Current Policies Related to Research for "Vulnerable" Populations?

Disability rights activists have long argued, "Nothing about us without us"—any decisions made *about* people with disabilities must take the diverse perspectives *of* people with disabilities into consideration. However, existing rules and regulations around doing research with people with disabilities makes it difficult to fulfill this important responsibility. This appendix addresses some methodological concerns related to conducting ethical research with people with disabilities, and offers suggestions for making this process easier while maintaining safety and confidentiality for participants.

Speaking with teenagers who had received special education services and been arrested for this study caused me to question and complicate some of my own assumptions about what schools should do, which is why it's necessary for researchers to continue talking with kids about their experiences with special education and the justice system. For example, when one participant first told me that they thought they should be allowed to come to school "high" (under the influence of marijuana), I initially disagreed. However, over time, I have come to realize that this young person was not arguing that being high would help them learn better, simply that it was not the "school's business" to suspend students who were high, since excluding students interfered with the "school's business" of providing academic opportunities. The school's decision to restrict kids' access to learning made the rule itself illegitimate in the student's eyes. I agree that this child would have likely learned more in a classroom under the influence of drugs than at they did at home. So, while I don't agree with the student's original argument that the school should just "let [them] be," when they come to school high, I can certainly see how the school's response did not lead to more and better learning opportunities for this student.

People with disabilities, children, and prisoners are all considered "vulnerable populations" and, as a result, researchers who want to speak with members of these groups have to clear many hurdles before doing so. Although well intentioned, these hurdles may have the counterproductive effect of deterring research that incorporates the perspectives of people most affected by particular policies and practices. In this appendix, I first offer recommendations for fellow researchers who want to conduct ethical research with "vulnerable populations" within the existing accountability landscape, then offer suggestions to the gatekeepers of this research to help promote more research that takes the perspectives of young people who have received special education services and/or been arrested into account and that still maintains safety and confidentiality for participants.

RECOMMENDATIONS FOR RESEARCHERS

This section offers two pieces of advice for researchers who want to learn more about the perspectives and experiences of "vulnerable populations."

First: build reciprocity into your study—participants in your study should benefit since the researcher will benefit from their participation. Not only is reciprocity an important ethical obligation of any research project but, as a bonus, doing the right thing can make your research better. Anyone who has experience in education, social work, youth development, and other related fields will have a lot to offer to any juvenile detention facility or program for people with disabilities that may be sites for recruiting participants or conducting studies. As a former middle and high school special education teacher, I tutored the students at Boys Home one night per week during the semester when I was recruiting and interviewing participants there. Other researchers have gone beyond that, leading drama workshops (see, e.g., Maisha T. Winn's excellent work) or supporting youth in developing critical research skills themselves (see, e.g., Michelle Knight-Manuel and Joanne E. Marciano's co-authored books that incorporate youth co-researchers).

Moving forward, I would like to conduct research that is more directly beneficial to participants. Approaches like participatory action research and youth participatory action research enlist participants as collaborators so that their concerns and interests are incorporated into the project, not just the researcher's. Supporting adolescents in conducting research can also help them become more critical consumers of research themselves, and even prepare them to conduct research in their own adult lives. Researchers can also reach out to adults who work in juvenile and other facilities to find out what questions they have that they want answered. Although the adults who helped me conduct this research project were uniformly supportive of my broader goals to disrupt the school-to-prison pipeline (STPP), they were also aware that my research didn't have many direct applications to their daily work, especially since many of these adults were working with kids who were already at the prison end of the STPP.

Reciprocity is an ethical obligation for any researcher, but, as a bonus, it has benefits for the researcher as well. Tutoring at Boys Home allowed me to better understand the context, and develop a deeper relationship with and understanding of young participants. Plus, I remembered how much I enjoyed being around teenagers with their goofy, sarcastic senses of humor. In the future, if I can conduct research that is more clearly and directly aligned with adults' needs, that will also reduce their work load since helping me out will more closely align with their existing duties. If I am helping staff solve more immediate problems they have, that will make their daily lives easier in the short term, which is important.

The second piece of advice I have for fellow researchers has to do with how to manage the exorbitant amounts of time it takes to conduct research with "vulnerable populations" within the realities of pressures to finish a dissertation, publish a certain number of articles each year, etc. Initially, I had to obtain approval from three Institutional Review Boards (IRBs): Teachers College (TC), The New York City Administration for Children's Services, and New York State Office of Child and Family Services (OCFS). These approvals needed to be obtained sequentially, in order. The process took one year to complete; I submitted my initial application to the full IRB at TC in December 2015, and obtained the final approval from OCFS on December 16, 2016. For one full year, there was nothing for me to do besides wait and twiddle my thumbs.

In order to continue conducting time-consuming research with "vulnerable populations" while also responding to pressures to publish research at a faster pace, I need to make sure that I have multiple studies in progress, with other studies using less time-consuming data sources. I would love to devote my time to working with young people receiving special education services who have been arrested, but need to balance that work with projects I can complete more quickly, such as those that involve interviewing adults or looking at texts. For researchers who are comfortable with quantitative research, a lot of data is publicly available and, as a result, can be accessed at any time. For example, most of the quantitative data I used for this study came from publicly available data, such as the data provided by the New York State Education Department, or from more easily obtainable data, such as data provided by the New York University Research Alliance, which I needed to request access to but did not require a full IRB process.

Although it's not possible to begin recruiting participants while awaiting approval, it is helpful to begin developing relationships with as many adults as possible and to get a sense of the context you will be working within so that you are ready to go as soon as you have received approval. For example, I had spoken extensively with the director of Boys Home, but I did not know any of the staff who worked there until the semester I began tutoring and recruiting there, so I did not fully understand the context of Boys Home. For example, Boys Home was frequently understaffed, with staff working double shifts to ensure that enough adults were present. Within this context, it is certainly understandable that helping to recruit participants for a stranger's research study was low priority. However, as I spent more time at Boys Home, I developed a better sense of the routines and schedules there, like when kids were likely to go on home visits. Knowing the routines allowed me to be more strategic about asking staff to send consent forms home.

RECOMMENDATIONS FOR GATEKEEPERS

There are, of course, good reasons that researchers have oversight from IRBs. However, having too many layers of oversight runs the risk of deterring research that incorporates student perspectives without any increase to student safety. Jumping through too many hoops can deter researchers and, paradoxically, pose a threat to research ethics by discouraging important research on understudied topics and groups. These recommendations maintain ethical standards while reducing redundancy and other sources of delays.

The first recommendation I would make is to allow researchers who have received approval from one institution's IRB to begin conducting research rather than requiring researchers to gain approval from multiple IRBs before beginning a research project. That would allow IRBs to engage in necessary oversight, but would not add excessive amounts of time to the approval process. If institutions are unwilling to accept the approval of another institution's IRB, they could still streamline the process and facilitate ethical research by allowing researchers to apply to all relevant IRBs concurrently rather than sequentially. Existing rules required me to submit my IRB application to my own institution first, wait for the full board to meet, make necessary revisions, resubmit, wait for approval—and then go through the same process two more times at two additional IRBs. There was a lot of down time while my applications were awaiting review (one full year between submitting the first application and receiving approval from the final IRB), and I could not use that time to even begin recruiting participants. Submitting my IRB to each institution at the same time would have significantly shortened the total amount of time I spent waiting.

A second recommendation is to allow for more nuance in the categories of research conducted with "vulnerable populations," just as there are different categories of research and approval used for adults. For example, the bar to clear if I want to ask teachers about their instructional decisions is much lower than what I would need to clear before I asked adults to take a new drug because these different types of research pose very different risks to participants. However, with children, people with certain types of disabilities, and prisoners, any type of research at all requires a very high-level of scrutiny and approval from the full IRB. In addition to addressing the risks that are present to any participant in a research study, this high-level of scrutiny exists because "vulnerable" populations are more vulnerable to coercion. With this in mind, IRB applications involving vulnerable populations should be required to demonstrate how they will reduce that risk in more detail but, otherwise, might not need as much oversight when they are engaging in activities that are considered to be of minimal risk to adults (e.g., asking about what someone likes best about a particular school).

A third recommendation is to allow for some exceptions to the requirement for parental consent when conducting research with kids who do not live at home. Even as a teacher, when my adolescent students were highly motivated to go on a particular field trip and lived at home with supportive, attentive adults, it was not uncommon for kids to forget to bring permission slips home in the first place, forget to get them signed, or forget to bring those signed slips back to school. When children are only seeing their parents or guardians occasionally and under high-stress situations (e.g., a court visit), it's not surprising that it is difficult to get consent forms signed. For research that poses no more than minimal risk, parents or guardians might be given a window of time to opt out and, certainly, every effort should be made to contact them to gain their affirmative consent. However, if an adolescent student is willing to participate and there is no reason to believe the family objects, certain types of research might be conducted after some time has passed without obtaining a permission slip. There is some precedent for this waiver in research where obtaining parental consent poses the greatest harm to a participant (e.g., research on abuse or research related to kids' reproductive health); the guidelines around ensuring that this research remains ethical could extend to kids who are living in residential facilities, where obtaining consent can be logistically prohibitive. Further, each IRB agreed that the main risk that my research posed to participants was the possibility that someone might identify participants and learn that they had been arrested as minors; with that in mind, collecting and holding consent forms, which used participants' and guardian's real names, was the activity that posed the largest risk to participants (since all other data was stored using only pseudonyms). Informed consent is absolutely important. However, if obtaining consent is so difficult as to actually discourage research with incarcerated kids with disabilities, then this becomes an ethical issue as well when all research conducted *on* this group is conducted without the input *of* this group.

A fourth recommendation is to allow researchers to recruit participants directly in ways that maintain participant confidentiality. For example, at Boys Home, I had to rely on overworked staff to recruit participants for me and to follow up with families so that I wouldn't know which kids had IEPs until they and their families had assented and consented to participate in my study. Understandably, recruiting participants for my study might fall by the wayside while staff were performing necessary functions. In the context of this research study, I could have made general recruitment presentations to all residents of Boys Home and distributed consent forms to everyone, then followed up to ensure eligibility after participants and their families consented (or did not refuse consent) to participate. For example, I might have been allowed to give a presentation to all of the boys at Boys Home and give consent forms to each without knowing any of their names, much less whether they had IEPs. For this study, I had to rely on the already overworked staff at Boys Home to send consent forms home and follow up with kids and their families.

DISCUSSION

Existing rules to protect "vulnerable populations," including minors, people with disabilities, and prisoners, run the risk of deterring researchers from conducting research that draws upon the valuable perspectives of kids, people with disabilities, and people who are court involved. Although well intentioned, existing research rules might cause harm to members of these groups by perpetuating policies and practices that do not benefit these groups. Research guidelines that systematically exclude or discourage the voices and perspectives of already marginalized groups are not ethical, and should be altered in ways that preserve safety for all research participants but still facilitate rather than hinder necessary research.

Appendix B
Study Methods

Data presented in this book came from a mixed methods study I conducted from 2015 to 2018. The purpose of this study was to better understand how schools seem to push certain young people, particularly those who have been previously identified for special education services, out of school and into prison. Although, as mentioned earlier in this book, much of the existing literature on this topic has looked for problems within individual children, there is evidence that school-level factors significantly influence this outcome. In other words, most existing research considers being identified as having a disability to be a student-level "risk factor" among many others that may predict poor outcomes, including getting arrested. However, school policies and practices affect the experiences and outcomes of students, including those receiving special education services.

This study focuses on the diverse and varied experiences of students with receiving special education services, and asks which school-level policies and practices may help or hinder students receiving special education services rather than assuming that the experience of being identified as having a disability is always the same or that disability is inherently "risky." Understanding school-level factors that predict arrest is important because those factors can be manipulated by educators and by policymakers at many levels, from individual classrooms to national policy. As a result, this study looked at how schools affect students rather than looking for supposed deficits within children.

I posed three questions for this study:

1. Which school-level factors predict arrest for young people who have received special educational services?

2. How do young people who have received special education services and been arrested present and explain these and other educational experiences that help or hinder them at school?
3. Where do the answers to these two questions converge and diverge?

In order to answer these questions, I used a QUAN, QUAL design (Creswell, 2014) in which the two strands served different, complementary purposes of equal importance to help me understand a complex phenomenon. The quantitative strand allowed me to understand, on a larger scale, which school-level factors predict arrest for young people who have received special education, on average, across New York City (Angrist & Pischke, 2009). The qualitative strand allowed me to understand, on a more local, contextualized level, how particular young people who have received special education services and been arrested present and explain those and other school-level factors that help or hinder them (Maxwell, 2013), including both experiences that converge with and diverge from the statistical average (Bogdan & Biklen, 2007). In the analysis, I looked at results that cross strands and results that are unique to each strand.

QUANTITATIVE DATA AND ANALYSIS

For the quantitative strand, I used regression analysis and administrative data from the New York City Department of Education (NYCDOE) and New York State Education Department (NYSED) to determine which school-level factors predicted an increased likelihood that students who have individualized education programs (IEPs) have been arrested over the course of one school year (Angrist & Pischke, 2009).

I constructed my dataset by aggregating student-level data from the NYCDOE and using school-level data from NYSED and the New York University Research Alliance for New York City Schools (Research Alliance) in order to construct a data set of school-level variables. I used data from each of the public secondary (middle and high) schools that the NYCDOE is responsible for, including traditional public schools, D75 schools, and charter schools for the most recent school year for which data were available (the 2013–2014 school year). The sample included 1,074 public middle and high schools run by the NYCDOE during the 2013–2014 school year. This data set does not include programs run by the NYCDOE that are not actually schools, such as tutoring programs for children in hospitals. I also excluded the two schools that only serve students who have already been arrested (East River Academy and Passages Academy).

Schools in NYC have varying organizational structures, with some serving students in grades K–8, 6–12, K-5, 6–8, 9–12, etc. When schools educated elementary school children as well as middle and high school children, my analyses only included information on students in grades 6–12 at that school. Many schools open and close each year in NYC, so some schools are in the process of adding or removing grades as they expand or get ready to shut down. This analysis includes schools that had served at least two grades from 6 to 12, since schools that are, for example, primarily elementary schools that have just added a sixth grade are likely to be different from many other secondary schools. Similarly, schools that are in the process of being closed for poor performance, that only offered one remaining class of students, are likely to be different in many ways from other public secondary schools.

District 75 schools, in particular, have unique organizational structures. They often have multiple school sites served by the same umbrella school organization. For example, 75K369 in Brooklyn runs programs in elementary schools, middle schools, and one high school. For the purpose of these analyses, 75K369 is treated as one school since it has one main principal and presumably shares characteristics across sites. In addition, the NYCDOE maintains data on these D75 schools as single schools. There is probably more diversity within D75 organizations than within other schools; however, I included D75 schools in my analyses since they are important sites for understanding the educational experiences of young people receiving special education services.

Unfortunately, the NYCDOE and NYSED do not collect the same data for different types of schools. As a result, I ran several rounds of analyses which included different types of schools and used different independent variables.

Variables

I chose independent variables related to a school's practice, context, and student demographics based on Raudenbush and Willms' (1995) conceptual framework that student outcomes are the result of school practice, school context, and student characteristics. Specific variables were selected based on my review of literature related to the STPP. Each variable is a school-level variable.

School Practice Variables

The variables related to a school's practice included: teachers' average number of years of experience; teachers' average annual number of days absent; percent of teachers with no valid certification; percent of teachers who turned over that year; percent of total students in collaborative team teaching classes; percent of total students in self-contained special education classes; percent of total students in alternative classes; high school dropout rates; school climate survey scores related to academic expectations, communication with families, student engagement, and school safety; percent of students who have been suspended at least once that year; pass rates on middle and high school Math and English Language Arts (ELA) examinations; and the total number of years the school has been in existence since NYU began collecting data in 1996.

Context Variables

Determining context variables within NYC is complex because students commute to schools all over the city for middle and high school rather than attending zoned neighborhood schools. As a result, the community that a school is physically located in does not necessarily reflect the community that students come from. For this set of variables, I looked at school classification (charter, D75, or traditional public school), and percent of students considered to be living in poverty (based on registration for FRPL or other benefits such as food stamps).

Student Characteristic Variables

Student characteristic variables included the racial demographics of the student body (percent of students who identify as Black, Latino, Asian/Pacific Islander, American Indian, Multiracial, or White), the percent of students who are formally classified as English Language Learners (ELLs), and the percent of students with IEPs. Although the purpose of this study was to examine school-level factors, student demographics were still relevant since research suggests that some factors will affect different groups of students differently. For example, the role of police in predominantly White and predominantly Black schools is very different.

Dependent Variable

The dependent variable used in each model was a dichotomous, school-level variable. If at least one student with an IEP had been arrested at a particular school, then that school was a "YesArrest" school (YesArrest = 1). If no students with IEPs had been arrested at a particular school, then that school was a "NoArrest" school (YesArrest = 0). Students were not necessarily arrested directly at their schools. However, school-level policies and practices may still lead to arrest indirectly. For example, students may be pushed out of school due to school-level practices and be at increased risk of arrest as a result of leaving school (see chapter 2 for a more detailed discussion of directly and indirectly risky school-level practices).

The dependent variable underestimates the true number of students who have received special education services and been arrested in NYC schools because the NYCDOE, NYSED, and the NYU Research Alliance do not maintain data on whether students have been arrested, but they do collect data on students who have been transferred to the particular D79 schools for young people who are detained awaiting trial or who have been sentenced to time at one of these facilities. Many young people who are arrested are not detained or placed in these D79 schools; instead, they might be released or referred to alternative-to-detention programs; the NYCDOE and NYSED do not have any data on these young people.

The dependent variable was dichotomous because the NYCDOE was not willing to release the total number of young people who had received special education services and been transferred to one of the relevant D79 schools when fewer than 10 students had been transferred. I only had data on whether students with IEPs had been transferred or not at 1,060 of the 1,074 schools, but did not know the exact number or percent.

ANALYTIC MODEL

Because my dependent variable was dichotomous (either students with IEPs at a particular school had been arrested or they had not), I used logistic regression to determine which school-level factors predicted an increased likelihood that a school would have students with IEPs who had been arrested.

My identifying equation was:

$$\log\left(\frac{Y_i}{1 - Y_i}\right) = \alpha + \beta_1 P_i + \beta_2 C_i + \beta_3 S_i + e_i$$

where Y_i is the dichotomous variable YesArrest; β_1 represents the effect of a vector of variables related to a school's practice; β_2 represents the effect of a vector of variables related to a school's context; and β_3 represents the effect of a vector of variables related to students' incoming characteristics.

I first ran descriptive analyses looking at differences between YesArrest schools and schools without arrests. Second, I ran a model with the most complete cases (1,073). Third, I removed variables that did not significantly predict a YesArrest school, and added variables related to teachers and test scores (N = 838). Fourth, I removed variables that did not significantly predict a YesArrest school and added the school climate survey scores (N = 841). Finally, I removed variables that did not significantly predict a YesArrest school and added the variable on how may total years the school had been in existence (N = 976).

For each model, I looked at goodness-of-fit tests, as well as for individual independent variables that statistically significantly predict an increased likelihood that a school will be a YesArrest school.

Missing Data

Missing data likely affected the results of this study, particularly because missing data was unlikely to be missing completely at random or even missing at random. Schools that maintain and report more complete student records are likely to be different in a variety of ways from schools whose records are less organized. For example, schools with incomplete records may have staff that is too overstretched and overwhelmed to maintain accurate records. These schools may also have higher arrest rates for young people receiving special education services.

In addition, at least some data in this study appeared to be inaccurate rather than missing. Specifically, some binary variables did not have any missing data and, as a result, clearly had some inaccuracies. For example, students were either classified as having a valid IEP (1) or not (0), but only 93 percent of students in D75 schools were classified as having a valid IEP, even though 100 percent were receiving special education services. One possibility is that many of those students' IEPs had expired—they did not, in fact, have valid IEPs. Another is that the data that were missing were simply coded as 0, or no IEP. As a result, it is difficult to understand the full extent of missing data on analyses in this study.

However, because the data set was constructed largely by student-level data aggregated to make school-level variables, it is more likely that a dysfunctional school is missing student data at random than that schools that are missing data are similar to schools which reported complete data sets. As a result, the effects of missing data may have been mitigated somewhat. Unfortunately, though, nonrandom missing data is a hazard of working with administrative data.

Analysis and Results

Because this study used logistic regression and SPSS, I used complete case analyses (Horton & Kleinman, 2007), meaning that each model only included schools with no missing data. For some variables, different types of schools had different types of data systematically missing, which is why I ran several different models, described earlier. For example, schools that were missing test score data were likely to be one of the 28 consortium schools whose students submit portfolio projects for graduation rather than take the Regents examinations. In addition, District 75 schools did not report school climate survey data, so the model using school climate survey data excluded D75 schools.

School-level data was compiled from student-level data, some of which may have been missing or inaccurate as well. School-level data from NYSED was based on data passed along from the NYCDOE, which received reports from individual schools, which vary in how they address missing data. When I created school-level variables from NYCDOE student-level data, I omitted missing data since schools with disorganized record keeping practices may not have systematically maintained poor records for students who are more or less likely to be arrested. On the one hand, students who have poor attendance or other characteristics that correlated with an increased likelihood of arrest may also have fewer data points to record; on the other hand, schools have incentives to keep careful records of students who are at risk of failing due to, for example, poor attendance, in case those schools get audited.

Model 1: The Most Complete Cases

The first round of analysis included the most complete cases and, as a result, excluded the most variables. This model included 1,073 of the 1,074 schools for which data were available, and included all traditional schools (n = 924), D75 schools (n = 54), and charter schools (n = 96).

According to the chi-square statistic, this model statistically significantly predicted an increased likelihood of a school being a YesArrest school (p = .000, < .05).

Because this study used logistic regression rather than ordinary least squares regression, I tested the fit of the model using the Hosmer–Lemeshow test rather than looking at the R^2 (Peng et al., 2002). The Hosmer–Lemeshow test suggested that the model is a good fit for the data (p = .137, > 0.05).

Model 2: Adding Test Data

State test score data was not available for all schools; as a result, this model included 841 schools. Most of the schools missing data were exempt from administering state tests for several reasons: (1) 28 schools are part of a consortium that administers alternative, portfolio-based assessments; (2) some D75 schools served only students who took the New York State Alternative Assessment rather than state standardized tests; and (3) some schools served students who were exempted from taking state tests, particularly in ELA because they were newly learning English. However, some schools were simply excluded from analysis because they had failed to report math and/or ELA test scores. Within schools that do administer state tests, some students are excluded from those tests because of their disabilities or ELL status.

With the exception of the 28 consortium schools, students are generally excluded from state tests on the assumption that students will not be able to pass those tests due to their disability or English proficiency. This presumed inability to pass the tests is assumed to reflect deficits within students resulting from their disabilities or their inability to speak fluent English rather than problems with the testing system or with the instruction they are receiving. Categorically excluding groups of students who have traditionally been marginalized within schools (students who are considered to have the most severe disabilities and novice ELLs) make it difficult to assess how well schools are educating *all* students. However, critiques about the ableist and culturally biased nature of large-scale assessments (e.g., Au, 2013; Harris-Murri et al., 2006; Hood, 1998; Lee, 1998; Solano-Flores & Nelson-Barber, 2001) reflect even greater difficulties in connecting these test scores directly to high-quality, culturally relevant instruction.

Student test score variables in this study were constructed from middle and high school ELA and Mathematics test score data. Students in grades 3–8 take state ELA and math exams each year. I used individual student data to construct pass rates for students in grades 6–8 at each school. A total of 633 schools had middle school test data. Students in grades 9–12 take Regents examinations in a variety of subjects, including ELA, math, science, and social studies. For high school students' test data, I used scores from the ELA Regents, taken in eleventh grade, and the Algebra 1 Regents, generally taken in ninth grade (but sometimes taken as early as eighth or as late as tenth grade). Although other math exams are available (e.g., Algebra II), Algebra I is the only examination that is mandatory for graduation, so Algebra I scores represent the broadest group of students; generally only more advanced students take additional Regents examinations. A total of 802 schools reported Algebra I scores, while 798 reported ELA Regents scores. Again, I created pass rates for each school based on the number of students who passed the test divided by the total number of students who had scores reported.

For schools that only administered middle or high school tests, these variables became the ELA or Math pass rate variables used in the study. For schools that reported both middle and high school variables, I averaged the pass rates for middle and high school tests to get the final ELA and Math pass rates. I chose to average the rates rather than calculating the pass rates based on individual student test scores because I wanted to weight the middle school and high school test scores equally. More middle school students than high school students take tests in a 6-12 school because middle school tests are administered each year in sixth to eighth grade, while high school tests are only administered once. However, I did not want to weight the middle school curriculum more heavily than the high school curriculum.

This model also statistically significantly predicted YesArrest schools (p = .000, < .05). However, the Hosmer–Lemeshow test suggests that this model is not a good fit for the data (p = .003, < .05). As a result, it is difficult to determine how useful this model is.

Model 3: Adding School Climate Survey Data

The third round of analyses also categorically excluded certain types of schools. Specifically, school climate survey data were not available for D75 or charter schools. The exclusion of D75 and charter schools is worrisome because both types of schools have unique relationships with students with IEPs. District 75 schools serve students with IEPs exclusively and, as such, are an important part of the educational landscape for children with disabilities in New York City. Charter schools in NYC have unique characteristics such as extremely high suspension rates (the top 39 suspension rates, and 47 of the top 50 suspension rates all belong to charter schools in this study) and a track record of educating a disproportionately low percent of students with disabilities (Rich, 2012), compared to noncharter public schools. School climate survey data stopped being collected in this format during the 2012–2013 school year, so the variables in this study are from the 2012–2013 school year rather than the 2013–2014 school year like the rest of the variables. This third model included 841 middle and high schools. This model statistically significantly predicted YesArrest schools ($p = .00, < .05$). This model was also a good fit for the data ($p = .468, > .05$).

Model 4: Adding School Age

New York City public schools underwent rapid change and restructuring in the decade leading up to this study as a result of No Child Left Behind and NYC mayor Michael Bloomberg's emphasis on small schools. As a result, most large and older NYC schools were closed and replaced with new, smaller schools. Policymakers hoped that these new, small schools would have better outcomes than the schools they replaced. Those who have attempted to evaluate the impacts of these new, small schools have run into trouble, though, because many of these small schools are selective, so they serve a different population of students than the schools they replaced, which had to educate all students within a particular geographic area. Nevertheless, I ran one last model looking to see whether a school's age predicted whether or not that school had students with IEPs who had been arrested. This data set does not include charter schools. However, most charter schools are newer, so it would be difficult to disentangle differences in the likelihood of a school being a YesArrest school that resulted from a school being newer from differences that result from a school being a charter school.

NYU's database included information on how many years the school had existed, starting in 1996. As a result, each school had been in existence for one to thirteen (or more) years during the 2013–2014 school year. It is important to note that older schools in this study were schools that had survived forced closures under NCLB and, as a result, are not necessarily representative of all older schools. For example, large and highly selective high schools such as the Bronx High School of Science were among the schools that had existed for at least thirteen years at the time of the study. This round of analyses included 976 schools.

This model statistically significantly predicted YesArrest schools (p = .000, < .05). However, this model was not a good fit for the data, making results difficult to interpret (p = .001, <.05).

QUALITATIVE DATA AND ANALYSIS

For the qualitative strand, I conducted semistructured interviews with seven young people (ages fifteen to twenty-one) who had received special education services and experienced arrest in NYC. Interviews allowed me to better understand how statistically significant school-level factors impact particular young people. In addition, I asked participants to identify and talk about school-level factors that are personally significant to them, that may predict arrest for particular young people receiving special education services.

I began recruiting participants by contacting the New York City Administration for Children's Services, which partners with multiple agencies to provide services for children under age sixteen (at the time of the study, now under the age of eighteen) who are in nonsecure and limited-secure detention or placement. One of these agencies agreed to recruit young people for my study. Through this agency, I became connected to a group home that I will call Boys Home, which housed a rotating group of 4–13 boys, mostly aged fourteen to sixteen, in a nonsecure setting. In order to protect the boys' privacy, staff determined which of the boys had received special education services, then reached out to the boys and their families to obtain assent and consent to participate. Only then was I introduced to the young people.

Recruiting participants in this way was difficult, and I was only able to interview two boys from Boys Home between December 2016 and June 2017. Due to the nature of the recruitment process, I'm not sure whether the difficulty in recruiting participants had to do with a low number of youth with IEPs; missing educational records; family or youth resistance to participation; youth forgetting to get consent forms signed on rare visits home; or staff not having time to pursue families among their many other duties.

Because of the difficulties associated with recruiting participants from Boys Home, I also reached out to individuals I knew who worked with young people with disabilities and/or court-involved youth to see if they knew anyone who might be interested in participating. I recruited four additional young people in this way. These adults included a lawyer and people who worked in schools in a variety of capacities (e.g., teachers, deans, counsellors). Youth aged eighteen to twenty-one gave consent; those under 18 obtained consent from their guardians and gave assent.

I conducted 1 to 3 semistructured interviews with each young person, ranging from 20 to 40 minutes in length. The purpose of these interviews was to ask participants to present and explain school experiences that enabled or disabled them at school. I began by asking open-ended questions to allow participant to identify topics of personal significance to them. Next, I asked them to speak about their experiences with topics that are statistically significant predictors of arrest in existing research or the quantitative stand of the study, such as the presence of police officers or high suspension rates.

Although I had hoped to conduct follow-up interviews and member checks with each participant, the nature of working with court-involved youth made that impossible in certain situations. For example, one participant was released from his group home a few days after our interview and, as a result, was not available for follow-up since the home, understandably, was not willing to release children's home contact information. Another older participant's cell phone ran out of minutes after our interview, making it impossible for either their lawyer or I to get in touch with them for a period of time, at which point the participant needed to return to an alternative boarding school out of town. I was ultimately able to conduct at least one longer interview (lasting at least 40 minutes) with each student, and additional follow-up interviews lasting 20–40 minutes with three of the seven students.

I coded data deductively, looking for themes related to ways in which schools enabled or disabled participants. I also coded data inductively, looking for codes and themes that were unique to my data, and for tensions within themes, ways in which different participants may have had differing experiences around a particular theme or had different experiences entirely (Bogdan & Biklen, 2007). For example, among the excerpts coded "relationships with adults," youth described a range of relationships from not remembering a teacher's name to saying that school staff were "family." I looked for areas of convergence and divergence with the quantitative results as well.

Data collection and analysis were iterative processes. For example, as I began to notice that participants seemed to buy into normative notions of what "regular" students and schools were supposed to look like and do, I followed up more carefully and thoroughly on the questions about advice for new students and teachers at a particular school to better understand how participants thought about what it took to be successful in those roles. I also developed and used the codes "normal student" and "regular teacher" in my coding.

ANALYSIS ACROSS STRANDS

Rather than using quantitative and qualitative methods primarily for triangulation, which generally relies only on convergent findings across methods and data sources (Marshall & Rossman, 2011), I used a mixed methods design to explore the complex problem of the STPP from many angles in order to see multiple facets of this problem (Calfee & Sperling, 2010). In analyzing data across both the quantitative and qualitative strands, I looked for areas of divergence as well as areas of convergence.

METHODOLOGICAL DIFFICULTIES AND AREAS FOR FUTURE RESEARCH

Because of the difficulty in recruiting participants and obtaining consent from their guardians, I interviewed the first seven young people who agreed to participate and returned signed consent forms. The process of recruiting and interviewing these seven young people took almost an entire year (December 2016–November 2017). The young people in this study all identified as Black and/or Latinx, English dominant, Christian, and heterosexual. Future research should also explore how young people receiving special education services who have been arrested and who come from other racial and linguistic backgrounds, religious minority groups, and/or who do not identify as heterosexual present and explain what helps and hinders them at school. In particular, two participants suggested that homophobia was present at their schools, but that they did not consider themselves directly affected by it. Girls were underrepresented in this study (two of seven participants) as they are in much research on the STPP because the Boys Home, but not the Girls Home, agreed to let me recruit participants. However, future research should continue to seek out the perspectives of girls and gender nonconforming youth.

In addition, future quantitative research on schools should consider alternative ways to quantify schools' curricula and academic rigor besides test scores. Initially, I had hoped to use data on student courses to better understand the offerings made available to students. For example, I hoped to see how many Advanced Placement classes were offered by high schools, and how many students were enrolled in those classes. However, students' courses are not reported in standardized ways, making comparisons across schools difficult. Further, some schools opt out of standardized tests and standardized curricula, such as Advanced Placement courses, altogether. The questions of how to quantify things like teaching and student learning are certainly not easy ones to answer.

Appendix C

Interview Questions

This appendix lists the questions that were asked during each interview with participants. In the interest of space, I have removed the framing of each interview and follow-up prompts that simply asked for more information (e.g., "what else . . . ?" or "can you give me an example of . . . ?" questions) or that clarified questions (e.g., "some ways that students might choose to identify are . . . do any of those words describe you, in your opinion?").

INTERVIEW # 1—GENERAL QUESTIONS ABOUT SCHOOL

General Information

How old are you?

What grade are you in now?

What school did you attend before attending [Passages Academy or East River Academy]?

How long were you a student there? What grades were you in?

[note: if less than one year, ask about previous school as well]

Why did you go to that school?

Can you tell me what it's like to be a student at [that school]?

What are some things you like best about your school?

What are some things you like least about your school?

What do you think are some differences between the school you went to and other schools?

If you could change some things about your school, what would they be?

If you met a kid who told you s/he was going to transfer to your school, what advice would you give her or him?

Is there anything you would like me to know about your school that we haven't talked about yet?

INTERVIEW #2—SCHOOL-LEVEL FACTORS

School-Level Factor: Teachers

Who was your favorite teacher?

    Why was s/he your favorite teacher?

    Can you tell me about a time this teacher did something you really liked?

Do you know how long this teacher taught at your school?

Were there any teachers you didn't like?

    Can you tell me about a teacher you didn't like?

    Why didn't you like this teacher?

    Can you tell me about a time this teacher did something you really didn't like?

If you met someone who was going to become a teacher at your school, what advice would you give him or her?

School-Level Factor: Police

Are there police or security guards who work at your school?

If yes: What do they do?

Have you ever interacted with the police or security guards at your school?

    If yes: What happened?

If no: What do you think about having police officers in a school? Is it a good idea?

    Do you know of any kids that go to school with police officers?

    If yes: Which school?

        What did they say about the police officers there?

There has been a lot in the news about police officers in schools. For example, did you see or hear about the video about the girl and the police officer in South Carolina?

    If yes: What did you think?

Do you think something like that could happen at your school?

School-Level Factor: Disciplinary Policies

Can you tell me about some of your schools' rules?

What happens if someone breaks a rule?
  Do you think that's fair? Why/why not?
Can you tell me about some policies or rules that you think are helpful or fair?
Can you tell me about some policies or rules that you think are not helpful or unfair?
What are some rules you wish your school had?
What are some rules you think your school should change?
Have you ever gotten in trouble at school?
  If yes: What happened?
  Why do you think you did that?
  What did the school do?
  Do you think that was a fair thing for the school to do?
    Why or why not?
  How did you feel when the school did that?

School-Level Factors: Resources

Does your school have a library? If yes: do you use it? If yes: What for?
Did you have a guidance counselor at your school?
  If yes: Did you ever talk to him/her?
    If yes: Did you decide to talk to him/her, or did you have to talk to him/her?
    How many times have you talked to him/her?
Was it about school or about a personal problem?
  Was your guidance counselor helpful? Why or why not?

School-Level Factor: Curriculum

What's your favorite class? Why?
What's your least favorite class? Why?
Do you get to choose any of your classes?
  If you could ask your school to offer a new class, what class would it be?
    What would you do in that class?
If middle school student:
  What do you know about the Regents exams?
  Do kids at your school take the Regents?
    If yes: In what subjects? Do most of them pass?
  Are you planning to take the Regents?
    If yes: In what subjects?
How is your school helping you prepare?
    If no: Why not?

If high school student:
   What do you know about advanced placement (AP) classes?
   Do kids at your school take AP classes?
      If yes: In what subjects? Do most of them pass?
   Are you planning to take AP classes?
      If yes: In what subjects?
How is your school helping you prepare?
   If no: Why not?

School-Level Factor: Restrictiveness of Special Education Services

What special education services did you receive?
What did you like or find helpful about [the services you received]?
What didn't you like or find helpful about [the services you received]?
Overall, are you glad you got these services?
   Why or why not?

School-Level Factor: Discrimination

Can you tell me about the kids in your school?
   Follow up: What race or ethnicity are most kids at your school?
What race and/or ethnicity would you use to describe yourself?
Do you think kids are ever treated unfairly because of their race at school?
What language do you speak at home with your family?
   [if language other than English]: Are there other kids at your school who
      speak this language at home also?
   Do you ever use that language at school? When? For what?
   Do you know any teachers at your school who speak this language?
   What other languages do kids at your school speak?
   [if languages other than English]: Do you know any teachers at your school
      who speak those languages?
Do you practice any particular religion?
   [if yes]: What religion?
   Do you ever feel like you have problems at school because of your religion?
What gender should I use to describe you?
   Do you think kids are ever treated unfairly because of their gender at
      school?
How would you describe your sexual orientation?
   Do you think kids are ever treated unfairly because of their sexual orienta-
      tion at school
Is there anything you would like to add about your school?

INTERVIEW #3—FOLLOW-UP AND MEMBER CHECKS

In interview [1/2], you said _____. What did you mean by that?

I want to make sure that I understand what you are trying to tell me. It sounds like you are saying x. Is that right?

When talking about _____, it seemed like you found _____ helpful, and _____ not so helpful. Is that correct?

[If participant indicates that anything is incorrect, I will say:] I'm sorry I misunderstood! Can you explain it to me again? [and then check again]

Is there anything that you have shared with me that you would rather I didn't tell anyone?

Is there anything you would like to add?

Do you have any questions for me?

References

Achilles, G. M., McLaughlin, M. J., & Croninger, R. G. (2007). Sociocultural correlates of disciplinary exclusion among students with emotional, behavioral, and
learning disabilities in the SEELS national dataset. *Journal of Emotional and
Behavioral Disorders*, *15*(33), 33–45. http://dx.doi.org/10.1177/10634266070
150010401.

Administration for Children's Services. (2014). *Youth and family justice.* http://www
.nyc.gov/html/acs/html/yfj/youth_family_justice.shtml.

American Civil Liberties Union. (2019). *Cops and no counselors: How the lack of
school mental health staff is harming students.* https://www.aclu.org/report/cops
-and-no-counselors.

Amrein-Beardsley, A. (2009). The unintended, pernicious consequences of "staying the course" on the United States' No Child Left Behind policy. *International
Journal of Education Policy & Leadership*, *4*(6), 1–13.

Angrist, J. D., & Pischke, J. S. (2009). *Mostly harmless econometrics: An empiricist's
companion.* Princeton University Press.

Annamma, S. A. (2018). Mapping consequential geographies in the carceral state:
Education journey mapping as a qualitative method with girls of color with dis/
abilities. *Qualitative Inquiry*, *24*(1), 20–34.

Annamma, S. A., Connor, D. J., & Ferri, B. (2013). Dis/ability critical race studies
(DisCrit): Theorizing at the intersections of race and dis/ability. *Race Ethnicity and
Education*, *16*(1), 1–31.

Anyon, Y., Gregory, A., Stone, S., Farrar, J., Jenson, J. M., McQueen, J., Downing,
B., Greer, E., & Simmons, J. (2016). Restorative interventions and school disci-
pline sanctions in a large urban school district. *American Educational Research
Journal*, *53*(6), 1663–1697.

Appleman, L. I. (2018). Deviancy, dependency, and disability: The forgotten history
of eugenics and mass incarceration. *Duke Law Journal*, *68*(3), 417–478.

Arya, N., Villarruel, F., Villanueva, C., & Augarten, I. (2009). *America's invisible children: Latino youth and the failure of justice.* The Campaign for Youth Justice and The National Council of La Raza.

Au, W. (2013). Hiding behind high-stakes testing: Meritocracy, objectivity and inequality in U.S. education. *The International Education Journal: Comparative Perspectives, 12*(2), 7–19.

Austistic Self Advocacy Network (ASAN). (2019). *Identify-first language.* https://autisticadvocacy.org/about-asan/identity-first-language/.

Bacher-Hicks, A., Billings, S. B., & Deming, D. J. (2019). *The school to prison pipeline: Long-run impacts of school suspensions on adult crime* (NBER Working Paper No. 26257). National Bureau of Economic Research. http://www.nber.org/papers/w26257.

Baglieri, S., Bejoian, L. M., Broderick, A. A., Connor, D. J., & Valle, J. (2011). [Re]claiming "inclusive education" toward cohesion in educational reform: Disability studies unravels the myth of the normal child. *Teachers College Record, 113*(10), 2122–2154.

Baglieri, S., Valle, J. W., Connor, D. J., & Gallagher, D. J. (2011). Disability studies in education: The need for a plurality of perspectives on disability. *Remedial and Special Education, 32*(4), 267–278.

Baker, B. (2002). The hunt for disability: The new eugenics and the normalization of school children. *Teachers College, 104*(4), 663–703.

Baynton, D. C. (2001). Disability and the justification of inequality in American history. In P. K. Longmore & L. Umansky (Eds.), *The new disability history: American perspectives.* NYU Press.

Berk, R. (2019). Accuracy and fairness for juvenile justice risk assessment. *Journal of Empirical Legal Studies, 16*(1), 175–194.

Bertrand, M., & Marsh, J. A. (2015). Teachers sensemaking of data and implications for equity. *American Educational Research Journal, 52*(5), 861–893.

Biklen, D., & Burke, J. (2006). Presuming competence. *Equity & Excellent in Education, 39*(2), 166–175.

Billups, A. B. (2009). *Classified.* https://www.youtube.com/watch?v=FX84jh5tlbM

Bissell-Brown, V. (1990). The fear of feminization: Los Angeles high schools in the progressive era. *Feminist Studies, 16,* 493–518.

Blake, J. J., Butler, B. R., Lewis, C. W., & Darensbourg, A. (2011). Unmasking the inequitable discipline experiences of urban black girls: Implications for urban educational stakeholders. *Urban Review, 43,* 90–106.

Blanchett, W. J. (2006). Disproportionate representation of African American students in special education: Acknowledging the role of White privilege and racism. *Educational Researcher, 35*(6), 24–28.

Blanchett, W. J., Klingner, J. K., & Harry, B. (2009). The intersection of race, culture, language and disability: Implications for urban education. *Urban Education, 44*(4), 389–409.

Blumenfeld, W. J. (2006). Christian privilege and the promotion of "secular" and not-so "secular" mainline Christianity in public schooling and in the larger society. *Equity & Excellence in Education, 39*(3), 195–210.

Board of Education of the Hendrick Hudson Central School District v. Rowley, 458 US 176 (1982).

Bogdan, R. C., & Biklen, S. K. (2007). *Qualitative research for education: An introduction to theory and methods.* Pearson.

Bracy, N. L. (2010). Circumventing the law: Students' rights in schools with police. *Journal of Contemporary Criminal Justice, 26*(3), 294–315.

Brantlinger, E. A. (2006). Winners need losers: The basis for school competition and hierarchies. In E. A. Brantlinger (Ed.), *Who benefits from special education? Remediating (fixing) other people's children.* Lawrence Erlbaum Associates.

Brown, B. (2005). Controlling crime and delinquency in the schools: An exploratory study of student perceptions of school security measures. *Journal of School Violence, 4*(4), 105–125.

Brown, S. J., Mears, D. P., Collier, N. L., Montes, A. N., Pesta, G. B., & Siennick, S. E. (2020). Education versus punishment? Silo effects and the school-to-prison pipeline. *Journal of Research in Crime and Delinquency, 57*(4), 403–443.

Burt, J. (2014). From zero-tolerance to compassion: Addressing the needs of girls caught in the school-to-prison pipeline through school-based mental health services. *Georgetown Journal of Law & Modern Critical Race Perspectives, 6*, 97–115.

Calfee, R., & Sperling, M. (2010). *On mixed methods.* Teachers College Press.

Carver-Thomas, D., & Darling-Hammond, L. (2017). *Teacher turnover: Why it matters and what we can do about it.* Learning Policy Institute.

CAST. (2020). *About universal design for learning.* http://www.cast.org/our-work/about-udl.html.

Christle, C. A., Jolivette, K., & Nelson, C. M. (2007). School characteristics related to high school dropout rates. *Remedial and Special Education, 28*(6), 325–339.

Cochran-Smith, M., Shakman, K., Jong, C., Terrell, D. G., Barnatt, J., & McQuillan, P. (2009). Good and just teaching: The case for social justice in teacher education. *American Journal of Education, 115*(3), 347–377.

Collins, K. M. (2011). Discursive positioning in a fifth-grade writing lesson: The making of a bad, bad boy. *Urban Education, 46*(4), 741–785.

Connor, D. J. (2009). Breaking containment: The power of narrative knowing: Countering silences within traditional special education research. *International Journal of Inclusive Education, 13*(5), 449–470.

Connor, D. J. (2013). Who "owns" dis/ability? The cultural work of critical special educators as insider-outsiders. *Theory & Research in Social Education, 41*(4), 494–513.

Connor, D. J., & Ferri, B. A. (2007). The conflict within: Resistance to inclusion and other paradoxes in special education. *Disability & Society, 22*(1), 63–77.

Crenshaw, K., Ocen, P., & Nanda, J. (2015). *Black girls matter: Pushed out, overpoliced and underprotected.* Columbia University Center for Intersectionality and Social Policy Studies.

Creswell, J. W. (2014). *Research design: Qualitative, quantitative, and mixed methods approaches.* SAGE.

Damore, S. J., & Murray, C. (2009). Urban elementary school teachers' perspectives regarding collaborative teaching practices. *Remedial and Special Education, 30*(4), 234–244.

Davis, A., Irvine, A., & Ziedenberg, J. (2014). *Close to home: Strategies to place young people in their communities.* National Council on Crime & Delinquency.

Deschennes, S., Cuban, L., & Tyack, D. (2001). Mismatch: Historical perspectives on schools and students who don't fit them. *Teachers College Record, 103*(4), 525–547.

Duncan-Andrade, J. M. R. (2009). Note to educators: Hope required when growing roses in concrete. *Harvard Educational Review, 79*(2), 181–194.

Eskenazi, M., Eddins, G., & Beam, J. M. (2003). *Equity or exclusion: The dynamics of resources, demographics, and behavior in the New York City public schools.* National Center for Schools and Communities.

Fabelo, T., Thompson, M. D., Plotkin, M., Carmichael, D., Marchanks, M. P., III., & Booth, E. A. (2011). *Breaking schools' rules: A statewide study of how school discipline relates to students' success and juvenile justice involvement.* Council of State Governments Justice Center.

Fallis, R. K., & Opotow, S. (2003). Are students failing school or are schools failing students? Class cutting in high school. *Journal of Social Issues, 59*(1), 103–119.

Fasching-Varner, K. J., Martin, L. L., Mitchell, R. W., Bennett-Haron, K. P., & Daneshzadeh, A. (Eds.). (2017). *Understanding, dismantling, and disrupting the prison-to-school pipeline.* Lexington Books.

Ferri, B. A., & Connor, D. J. (2010). "I was the special ed. girl": Urban working-class young women of colour. *Gender and Education, 22*(1), 105–121.

Frederick, A., & Shifrer, D. (2019). Race and disability: From analogy to intersectionality. *Sociology of Race and Ethnicity, 5*(2), 200–214.

Fuchs, D., Fuchs, L. S., & Vaughn, S. (2014). What is intensive instruction and why is it important? *Teaching Exceptional Children, 46*(4), 13–18.

Gage, N. A., Josephs, N. L., & Lunde, K. (2012). Girls with emotional disturbance and a history of arrest: Characteristics and school-based predictors of arrest. *Education and Treatment of Children, 35*(4), 603–622.

Gallagher, D. J. (2004). Entering the conversation: The debate behind the debates in special education. In D. J. Gallagher, L. Heshusius, R. P. Iano, & T. M. Skrtic (Eds.), *Challenging orthodoxy in special education: Dissenting voices* (pp. 3–26). Love Publishing Company.

Gay, G. (2010). *Culturally responsive teaching: Theory, research & practice.* Teachers College Press.

Glaberson, W. (2010, April 27). Lessons in tough love at a court for truants. *The New York Times.* http://www.nytimes.com/2010/04/28/nyregion/28truant.html.

Goodman, J. (2014). *Flaking out: Student absences and snow days as disruptions of instructional time* (NBER Working Paper No. 20221). National Bureau of Economic Research. http://www.nber.org/papers/w20221.

Gregory, A., Clawson, K., Davis, A., & Gerewitz, J. (2016). The promise of restorative practices to transform teacher-student relationships and achieve equity in school discipline. *Journal of Educational and Psychological Consultation, 26*(4), 325–353.

Gregory, A., & Ripski, M. B. (2008). Adolescent trust in teachers: Implications for behavior in the high school classroom. *School Psychology, 37*(3), 337–353.

Gregory, A., Skiba, R. J., & Noguera, P. A. (2010). The achievement gap and the discipline gap: Two sides of the same coin? *Educational Researcher, 39*(1), 59–68.

Hanselman, P., & Fiel, J. E. (2017). School opportunity hoarding? Racial segregation and access to high growth schools. *Social Forces, 95*(3), 1077–1104.

Harris-Murri, N., King, K., & Rostenberg, D. (2006). Reducing disproportionate minority representation in special education programs for students with emotional disturbances: Toward a culturally responsive response to intervention model. *Education and Treatment of Children, 29*(4), 779–799.

Harry, B., & Fenton, P. (2016). Risk in schooling: The contribution of qualitative research to our understanding of the overrepresentation of minorities in special education. *Multiple Voices for Ethnically Diverse Exceptional Learners, 16*(1), 17–28.

Harry, B., & Klingner, J. K. (2006). *Why are so many minority students in special education?: Understanding race & disability in schools.* Teachers College Press.

Havik, T., Bru, E., & Ertesvag, S. K. (2015). School factors associated with school refusal and truancy-related reasons for school non-attendance. *Social Psychology of Education, 18*, 221–240.

Hehir, T. (2002). Eliminating ableism in education. *Harvard Educational Review, 72*(1), 1–32.

Hines-Datiri, D., & Andrews, D. J. C. (2020). The effects of zero tolerance policies on Black girls: Using critical race feminism and figured worlds to examine school discipline. *Urban Education, 55*(10), 1419–1440.

Hirschfield, P. J. (2008). Preparing for prison? The criminalization of school discipline in the USA. *Theoretical Criminology, 12*(1), 79–101.

Hirschfield, P. J. (2018). The role of schools in sustaining juvenile justice system inequality. *The Future of Children, 28*(1), 11–35.

Hoogland, I., Schildkamp, K., van der Kleij, F., Heitink, M., Kippers, W., Veldkamp, B., & Dijkstra, A. M. (2016). Prerequisites for data-based decision making in the classroom: Research evidence and practical illustrations. *Teaching and Teacher Education, 60*, 377–386.

Hopper, F. (2016, December 29). Fighting the worst pipeline of all: From school to prison. *Indian Country Today.* https://indiancountrytoday.com/archive/fighting-the-worst-pipeline-of-all-from-school-to-prison-kYyNgXmPTku1x1JLEKfM4w.

Horn, C. (2003). High-stakes testing and students: Stopping or perpetuating a cycle of failure? *Theory into Practice, 42*(1), 30–41.

Horton, N. J., & Kleinman, K. P. (2007). Much ado about nothing. *The American Statistician, 61*(1), 79–90.

Hunt, J., & Moodie-Mills, A. (2012). *The unfair criminalization of gay and transgender youth: An overview of the experiences of LGBT youth in the juvenile justice system.* Center for American Progress. https://www.americanprogress.org/issues/lgbtq-rights/reports/2012/06/29/11730/the-unfair-criminalization-of-gay-and-transgender-youth/.

Individuals with Disabilities Education Act, 20 U.S.C. § 1400 (2004).

Ingalls, L., Hammond, H., & Trussell, R. P. (2011). An evaluation of past special education programs and services provided to incarcerated young offenders. *The Journal of At-Risk Issues, 16*(2), 25–32.

Irby, D. J. (2013). Net-deepening of school discipline. *Urban Review, 45*, 197–219.

Jung, P., Cendana, G., Chiang, W., Wang, B., Zheng, E., Thammarath, M., Dinh, Q., & Mariategue, K. D. (2015). *Asian Americans & Pacific Islanders behind bars: Exposing the school to prison to deportation pipeline.* Asian Americans Advancing Justice.

Kauffman, J. M., & Badar, J. (2014). Instruction, not inclusion, should be the central issue in special education: An alternative view from the USA. *Journal of International Special Needs Education, 17*(1), 13–20.

Kauffman, J. M., Bantz, J., & McCullough, J. (2002). Separate and better: A special public school class for students with emotional and behavioral disorders. *Exceptionality, 10*(3), 149–170.

Kemple, J. (2015). *High school closures in New York City: Impacts on students' academic outcomes, attendance, and mobility.* The Research Alliance for New York City Schools.

Kim, C., Losen, D., & Hewitt, D. (2010). *The school-to-prison pipeline: Structuring legal reform.* New York University Press.

Kliebard, H. M. (1987). *The struggle for the American curriculum, 1893–1958.* Routledge.

Kliewer, C. (1998). *Schooling children with Down Syndrome: Toward an understanding of possibility.* Teachers College Press.

Knight, M. G., & Marciano, J. E. (2013). *College ready: Preparing Black and Latina/o youth for higher education—A culturally relevant approach.* Teachers College Press.

Kramarczuk Voulgarides, C., Fergus, E., & King Thorius, K. A. (2017). Pursuing equity: Disproportionality in special education and the reframing of technical solutions to address systemic inequities. *Review of Research in Education, 41*, 61–87.

Kumashiro, K. (2001). *Troubling education: Queer activism and anti-oppressive pedagogy.* Routledge.

Ladson-Billings, G. (1995). Toward a theory of culturally relevant pedagogy. *American Educational Research Journal, 32*(3), 465–491.

Ladson-Billings, G. (2006). From the achievement gap to the education debt: Understanding achievement in U.S. schools. *Educational Researcher, 35*(7), 3–12.

Ladson-Billings, G. (2014). Culturally relevant pedagogy 2.0: A.k.a. the remix. *Harvard Educational Review, 84*(1), 74–84.

Link, B. G., & Phelan, J. C. (2001). Conceptualizing stigma. *Annual Review of Sociology, 27*, 363–385.

Lyken-Segosebe, D., & Hinz, S. E. (2015). The politics of parental involvement: How opportunity hoarding and prying shape educational opportunity. *Peabody Journal of Education, 90*(1), 93–112.

Mallett, C. A. (2014). The learning disabilities to juvenile detention pipeline: A case study. *Children & Schools, 36*(3), 147–154.

Marshall, C., & Rossmann, G. B. (2011). *Designing qualitative research.* SAGE Publications.

Maxwell, J. A. (2013). *Qualitative research design: An interactive approach.* SAGE Publications.

McGrew, K. (2016). The dangers of pipeline thinking: How the school-to-prison pipeline metaphor squeezes out complexity. *Educational Theory, 66*(3), 341–367.

McIntosh, K., Girvan, E. J., Horner, R. H., Smolkowski, K., & Sugai, G. (2018). *A 5-point intervention approach for enhancing equity in school discipline.* http://www.pbis.org/Common/Cms/files/pbisresources/A%205-Point%20 Intervention %20%20Approach%20for%20Enhancing%20%20Equity%20in%20School %20Discipline.pdf.

McKenna, J. M., & White, S. R. (2018). Examining the use of police in schools: How roles may impact responses to student misconduct. *American Journal of Criminal Justice, 43*, 448–470.

Migliarini, V., & Annamma, S. A. (2020). Classroom and behavior management: (Re)conceptualization through disability critical race theory. In R. Papa (Ed.), *Handbook on promoting social justice in education* (pp. 1511–1532). Springer.

Mittleman, J. (2018). Sexual orientation and school discipline: New evidence from a population-based sample. *Educational Researcher, 47*(3), 181–190.

Murphy, A. S., Acosta, M. A., & Kennedy-Lewis, B. L. (2013). "I'm not running around with my pants sagging, so how am I not acting like a lady?": Intersections of race and gender in the experiences of female middle school troublemakers. *Urban Review, 45*, 586–610.

Murray, C., & Pianta, R. C. (2007). The importance of teacher-student relationships for adolescents with high incidence disabilities. *Theory into Practice, 46*(2), 105–112.

Nanda, J. (2019). The construction and criminalization of disability in school incarceration. *Columbia Journal of Race and Law, 9*(2), 265–322.

National Association of Secondary School Principals. (2006). *Tracking and ability grouping in middle level and high schools.* https://www.nassp.org/policy-advocacy -center/nassp-position-statements/archived-position-statements/tracking-and-abil-ity-grouping-in-middle-level-and-high-schools/.

National Center for Education Statistics. (2016). *Fast facts: Students with disabilities, inclusion of.* https://nces.ed.gov/fastfacts/display.asp?id=59.

National Center for Education Statistics. (2017). *Fast facts: Back to school statistics.* https://nces.ed.gov/fastfacts/display.asp?id=372.

National Commission. (1983). *A nation at risk: The imperative for educational reform.* http://www2.ed.gov/pubs/NatAtRisk/index.html.

National Council on Disability. (2018). *The segregation of students with disabilities.* https://ncd.gov/publications/2018/individuals-disabilities-education-act-report -series-5-report-briefs.

Nelson-Barber, S., & Trumbull, E. (2007). Making assessment practices valid for Indigenous American students. *Journal of American Indian Education, 46*(3), 132–147.

New York City Department of Education (NYCDOE). (2009). *ChildrenFirst: A bold, common-sense plan to create great schools for all New York City children.* http://schools.nyc.gov/NR/rdonlyres/51C61E8F-1AE9-4D37-8881-4D688D4F843A/0/cf_corenarrative.pdf.

New York City Department of Education. (2019). *Report on guidance counselors pursuant to local law 56 of 2014.* https://infohub.nyced.org/reports/government-reports/guidance-counselor-reporting.

New York City Independent Budget Office (NYCIBO). (2014). *Demographics and work experience: A statistical portrait of New York City's public school teachers.* New York City Independent Budget Office.

New York Civil Liberties Union. (2013). *A, B, C, D, STPP: How school discipline feeds the school-to-prison pipeline.* http://www.nyclu.org/publications/report-b-c-d-stpp-how-school-discipline-feeds-school-prison-pipeline-2013.

New York Civil Liberties Union. (2018). *Student safety act reporting 2018.* https://www.nyclu.org/en/student-safety-act-data.

New York Civil Liberties Union. (2019a). *Student safety act reporting 2019.* https://www.nyclu.org/en/student-safety-act-data.

New York Civil Liberties Union. (2019b). *New report shows shortage of counselors, over-policing, and discriminatory discipline in schools in New York.* https://www.nyclu.org/en/press-releases/new-report-shows-shortage-counselors-over-policing-and-discriminatory-discipline.

New York State Education Department (NYSED). (2014). *NYC Spec schools: Dist 75 enrollment (2013–14).* http://data.nysed.gov/enrollment.php?year=2014&instid=800000057444.

New York State Education Department (NYSED). (2015). *Special education state performance plan.* http://www.p12.nysed.gov/specialed/spp/.

Oakes, J. (2005). *Keeping track: How schools structure inequality.* Yale University Press.

Office of Child and Family Services (OCFS). (2015). *Close to home initiative.* http://ocfs.ny.gov/main/rehab/close_to_home/.

O'Neil, C. (2017). *Weapons of math destruction.* Crown Publishing Group.

Osgood, R. L. (1997). Undermining the common school ideal: Intermediate schools and ungraded classes in Boston, 1838–1900. *History of Education Quarterly, 37*(4), 375–398.

Paris, D., & Alim, H. S. (2014). What are we seeking to sustain through culturally sustaining pedagogy? A loving critique forward. *Harvard Educational Review, 84*(1), 85–100.

Patall, E. A., Cooper, H., & Allen, A. B. (2010). Extending the school day or school year: A systematic review of research (1985–2009). *Review of Educational Research, 80*(3), 401–436.

Peng, C. J., Lee, K. L., & Ingersoll, G. M. (2002). An introduction to logistic regression analysis and reporting. *The Journal of Educational Research, 96*(1), 3–14.

Price, P. (2009). When is a police officer an officer of the law?: The status of police officers in schools. *The Journal of Criminal Law & Criminology, 99*(2), 541–570.

Ramey, D. M. (2015). The social structure of criminalized and medicalized school discipline. *Sociology of Education, 88*(3), 181–201.

Raudenbush, S. W., & Willms, J. D. (1995). The estimation of school effects. *Journal of Educational and Behavioral Statistics, 20*(4), 307–335.

Reid, D. K., & Knight, M. G. (2006). Disability justifies exclusion of minority students: A critical history grounded in disability studies. *Educational Researcher, 35*(6), 18–23.

Research Alliance for New York City Schools. (2016). *School-level master file 1996* [Data file and code book]. Unpublished data.

Rich, M. (2012, June 19). Charter schools still enroll fewer disabled students. *The New York Times.* http://www.nytimes.com/2012/06/20/education/in-charter -schools-fewer-with-disabilities.html.

Richardson, J. G. (1994). Common, delinquent, and special: On the formalization of common schooling in the American states. *American Educational Research Journal, 31*(4), 695–723.

Riehl, C. J., Earle, H., Nagarajan, P., Schwitzman, T. E., & Vernikoff, L. (2018). Following the path of greatest persistence: Sensemaking, data use, and the everyday practice of teaching. In. N. Barnes & H. Fives (Eds.), *Cases of teachers' data use* (pp. 30–43). Routledge.

Rivera, E. A., McMahon, S. D., & Keys, C. B. (2014). Collaborative teaching: School implementation and connections with outcomes among students with disabilities. *Journal of Prevention & Intervention in the Community, 42*(1), 72–85.

Rocque, M., Jennings, W. G., Piquero, A., Ozkan, T., & Farrington, D. P. (2017). The importance of school attendance: Findings from the Cambridge study in delinquent development on the life-course effects of truancy. *Crime and Delinquency, 63*(5), 592–612.

Rocque, M., & Paternoster, R. (2011). Understanding the antecedents of the "school-to-jail" link: The relationship between race and school discipline. *The Journal of Criminal Law & Criminology, 101*(2), 633–665.

Rocque, M., & Snellings, Q. (2018). The new disciplinology: Research, theory, and remaining puzzles on the school-to-prison pipeline. *Journal of Criminal Justice, 59*, 3–11.

Roegman, R., Pratt, S., Sanchez, S., & Chen, C. (2018). Between extraordinary and marginalized: Negotiating tensions in becoming special education-certified teachers. *The New Educator, 14*(4), 293–314. http://dx.doi.org/10.1080/1547688X.2017 .1287317.

Rosenbaum, J. (2018). Educational and criminal justice outcomes 12 years after school suspension. *Youth & Society, 52*(4), 515–547.

Rubin, B. C. (2003). Unpacking detracking: When progressive pedagogy meets students' social worlds. *American Educational Research Journal, 40*(2), 539–573.

Salmon, N. (2013). 'We just stick together': How disabled teens negotiate stigma to create lasting friendship. *Journal of Intellectual Disability Research, 57*(4), 347–358.

Sharpe, G., & Gelsthorpe, L. (2009). Engendering the agenda: Girls, young women and youth justice. *Youth Justice, 9*(3), 195–208.

Shifrer, D. (2013). Stigma of a label: Educational expectations for high school students labeled with learning disabilities. *Journal of Health and Social Behavior, 54*(4), 462–480.

Singer, N. (2016, January 23). An app helps teachers track student attendance. *The New York Times*. https://www.nytimes.com/2016/01/24/technology/an-app-helps -teachers-track-student-attendance.html.

Skiba, R. (2002). Special education and school discipline: A precarious balance. *Behavioral Disorders, 27*(2), 81–97.

Skiba, R. J., Arredondo, M. I., & Williams, N. T. (2014). More than a metaphor: The contribution of exclusionary discipline to a school-to-prison pipeline. *Equity & Excellence in Education, 47*(4), 546–564.

Sleeter, C. E. (1986). Learning disabilities: The social construction of a special education category. *Exceptional Children, 53*(1), 46–54.

Smalls, C., White, R., Chavous, T., & Sellers, R. (2007). Racial ideological beliefs and racial discrimination experiences as predictors of academic engagement among African American adolescents. *Journal of Black Psychology, 33*(3), 299–330.

Smyth, J. (2007). Toward the pedagogically engaged school: Listening to student voice as a positive response to disengagement and 'dropping out'? In D. Thiessen & A. Cook-Sather (Eds.), *International handbook of student experience in elementary and secondary school* (pp. 635–658). Springer.

Snyder, S. L., & Mitchell, D. T. (2006). *Cultural locations of disability*. The University of Chicago Press.

Solano-Flores, G., & Nelson-Barber, S. (2001). On the cultural validity of science assessments. *Journal of Research in Science Teaching, 38*(5), 553–573.

Sprague, J. R., Vincent, C. G., Tobin, T. J., & CHiXapkaid. (2013). Preventing disciplinary exclusions of students from American Indian/Alaska Native backgrounds. *Family Court Review, 51*(3), 452–459.

Spring, J. (1989). *The sorting machine revisited*. Longman.

Stern, M., Clonan, S., Jaffee, L., & Lee, A. (2015). The normative limits of choice: Charter schools, disability studies, and questions of inclusion. *Educational Policy, 29*(3), 448–477.

Stiefel, L., Shiferaw, M., Schwartz, A. E., & Gottfried, M. (2017). *Is special education improving? Evidence on segregation, outcomes, and spending from New York City* (IESP Working Paper #02-17). NYU Steinhardt Institute for Education and Social Policy. https://steinhardt.nyu.edu/scmsAdmin/media/users/lwb232/ Is_Special_Education_Improving_Evidence_on_Segregation_Outcomes_and _Spending_from_New_York_City.pdf.

Stillman, J. (2011). Teacher learning in an era of high-stakes accountability: Productive tension and critical professional practice. *Teachers College Record, 113*(1), 133–180.

Stinchcomb, J. B., Bazemore, G., & Riestenberg, N. (2006). Beyond zero tolerance: Restoring justice in secondary schools. *Youth Violence and Juvenile Justice, 4*(2), 123–147.

Stokes, S. B. S. (2011). *The relationship between suspension, student engagement, and dropout* (Doctoral Dissertation). ProQuest. (3457217).

Terzi, L. (2007). Capability and educational equality: The just distribution of resources to students with disabilities and special educational needs. *Journal of Philosophy of Education, 41*(4), 757–773.

Thompson, W. C., Beneke, A. J., & Mitchell, G. S. (2020). Legitimate concerns: On complications of identity in school punishment. *Theory and Research in Education, 18*(1), 78–97.

Tierney, W. G., & Colyar, J. E. (2005). The role of peer groups in college preparation programs. In W. G. Tierney, Z. B. Corwin, & J. E. Colyar (Eds.), *Preparing for college: Nine elements of effective outreach* (pp. 49–68). State University of New York Press.

Togut, T. D. (2011). The gestalt of the school-to-prison pipeline: The duality of overrepresentation of minorities in special education and racial disparity in school discipline on minorities. *Journal of Gender, Social Policy & the Law, 20*(1), 163–181.

Tyack, D., & Cuban, L. (1995). *Tinkering toward Utopia.* Harvard University Press.

Tyack, D., & Hansot, E. (1992). *Learning together: A history of coeducation in American public schools.* Russell Sage Foundation.

Tyack, D. B. (1974). *The one best system: A history of American urban education.* Harvard University Press.

United States Department of Education. (2015). *Laws & guidance.* http://www2.ed.gov/policy/landing.jhtml?src=pn.

Utley, C. A., Kozleski, E., Smith, A., & Draper, I. L. (2002). Positive behavior support: A proactive strategy for minimizing behavior problems in urban multicultural youth. *Journal of Positive Behavior Interventions, 4*(4), 196–207.

Valenzuela, A. (1999). *Subtractive schooling: U.S.-Mexican youth and the politics of caring.* State University of New York Press.

Valle, J. W., & Connor, D. J. (2011). *Rethinking disability: A disability studies approach to inclusive practices.* McGraw Hill.

Viadero, D. (2005). Uniform effects? Schools cite benefits of student uniforms, but researchers see little evidence of effectiveness. *Education Week, 24*(18), 27–29.

Villalpondo, O., & Solarzano, D. (2005). The role of culture in college preparation programs: A review of the research literature. In W. G. Tierney, Z. B. Corwin, & J. E. Colyar (Eds.), *Preparing for college: Nine elements of effective outreach* (pp. 13–28). State University of New York Press.

Waitoller, F. R., & Thorius, K. A. K. (2016). Cross-pollinating culturally sustaining pedagogy and universal design for learning: Toward an inclusive pedagogy that accounts for dis/ability. *Harvard Educational Review, 86*(3), 366–389.

Warnick, B. R., & Scribner, C. F. (2020). Discipline, punishment, and the moral community of schools. *Theory and Research in Education, 18*(1), 98–116.

Weiss, R. S. (1994). *Learning from strangers: The art and method of qualitative interview studies.* Free Press.

Welsh, R. O., & Little, S. (2018). The school discipline dilemma: A comprehensive review of disparities and alternative approaches. *Review of Educational Research, 88*(5), 752–794.

Wilson, M. G. (2014). Disrupting the pipeline: The role of school leadership in mitigating exclusion and criminalization of students. *Journal of Special Education Leadership, 26*(2), 61–70.

Winn, M. T. (2011). "We try to find our way home": Formerly incarcerated girls speak up. In *Girl time: Literacy, justice, and the school-to-prison pipeline* (pp. 67–105). Teachers College Press.

Winn, M. T., & Behizadeh, N. (2011). The right to be literate: Literacy, education, and the school-to-prison pipeline. *Review of Research in Education, 35*, 147–173.

Wolff, C. E., Jarodzka, H., & Boshuizen, H. P. A. (2017). See and tell: Differences between expert and novice teachers' interpretations of problematic classroom management events. *Teaching and Teacher Education, 66*, 295–308.

Yeung, R. (2009). Are school uniforms a good fit? Results from the ECLS-K and the NELS. *Educational Policy, 23*(6), 847–874.

Youdell, D. (2006). *Impossible bodies, impossible selves: Exclusion and student subjectivities.* Springer.

Index

Page references for figures are italicized.

About the Author

Laura Vernikoff is an assistant professor of special education at Touro College Graduate School of Education, and a former middle and high school special education teacher. She is a graduate of New York City public schools, Johns Hopkins University, and the Pennsylvania State University. She received her doctorate in Curriculum and Teaching from Teachers College, Columbia University. Her research interests include inclusive education and the many strengths and advantages of urban communities and urban education.

www.ingramcontent.com/pod-product-compliance
Lightning Source LLC
Chambersburg PA
CBHW050612280326
41932CB00016B/3016